MISSION STATEMENTS

JAMES BOND AT THE MOVIES

NICK SETCHFIELD

CONTENTS

"I ADMIRE YOUR LUCK, MR..?"

An introduction

The first James Bond film I ever saw was *From Russia With Love*, an ITV screening when I was eight years old. It felt like a rite of passage, unlocking a wider, more thrilling world.

Bond was in my consciousness before then, of course. But I knew that he belonged to the universe of older kids and grown-ups, the universe you were required to earn admittance to. Unlike Doctor Who or Batman, Bond's exploits lived exclusively in my imagination, fuelled by glimpses and whispers, pictures and rumours, tantalising promises of violence and sex and diabolical strangeness. The good stuff. A friend at school had the poster magazine for *The Man With The Golden Gun* (I can't remember if he'd actually seen the movie). He let me borrow it and I pored over every word and photograph, on a contact high from such playground contraband.

So to finally see a Bond adventure was a major deal. *From Russia With Love* isn't one of the more kid-friendly films in the series but I was spellbound just the same. There were poison-tipped switch-blade shoes and Siamese fighting fish and secret caverns beneath Istanbul. Above all there was 007, a hero whose style, whose bulletproof cool, whose entire, fantastic milieu clearly eclipsed his closest rivals. When the film was over my response was immediate: "Dad, he's better than Kojak!"

My big-screen baptism came in the summer of 1977. We were on holiday in London and the Underground was emblazoned with posters for Bond's latest adventure, *The Spy Who Loved Me*. I saw them as soon as we arrived. I remember these posters as being outsized, perhaps the length of four standard posters, possibly even four whole walls of the Tube. That can't be right; perhaps that was simply the amount of excitement they struggled to contain as they promised "It's the biggest. It's the best. It's Bond. And beyond." Spotting a sleek white sports car slicing through the sea I knew I needed to see this film, as soon as humanly possible, if not a great deal sooner.

"We're not spending our holiday in the cinema," said my father, firmly. And so I trotted patiently through tourist attractions for the next couple of days, the thought of that Bond film itching away with all its oversized promise. That car. That beautiful, impossible car...

That Wednesday afternoon, riding the Tube once more, my dad withheld our destination. It was going to be a surprise. Even when we arrived in Leicester Square I had no real notion of what Leicester Square could be. And then I saw the Odeon. And the poster for *The Spy Who Loved Me*. It was the biggest cinema I had ever been in. And the biggest film I had ever seen. Big as dreams, bright and brilliant in the dark. The trailer for *Star Wars* was simply the icing.

The Bond movies were in my bloodstream now. Instinctively I wanted to contextualise it all. That summer Look-In magazine celebrated the release of *Spy* with a potted history of the films. There, wedged between pictures of Roger Moore ("the latest 007") and Sean Connery ("pioneer Bond") was a pensive-looking, previously unsuspected figure named George Lazenby. He had, apparently, taken one shot at Bond and blown it. His picture radiated an intriguing air of melancholy and mystique. Soon after I found secondhand copies of two of Fleming's original novels, Dr. No and From Russia With Love. Their grey, musty pages felt like archaeological treasure in my hands. Dr. No was a tie-in edition to the film's 1962 release. Connery was on the cover, held at gunpoint by Steve McGarrett from *Hawaii Five-0.*

ITV continued to show the Connery adventures (one night I had an anxiety dream I'd forgotten *Goldfinger* was on; a very real existential terror in the days before any movie was simply a click or a shelf away). After each film I felt a distinct Bond-buzz, an intoxication I never quite experienced with any other entertainment. I'd play on the stairs in the dark, pretending they were Fort Knox or Nassau, Bond's world heady inside me.

I loved these films. I still do.

In my career as a writer Bond's been a constant thread. He's tailed me. Or maybe I've tailed him. My first professional sale was an article on George Lazenby in 1991 (I was still intrigued). As features editor on SFX I visited Pinewood's legendary 007 Stage for the press launch of *Die Another Day* in 2002. Later that afternoon, loitering in a corridor with another journalist, I saw Pierce Brosnan, suited and booted, burst through double-doors and stride past us, trailing personal assistants in his wake. It felt like virtual reality. That same year I interviewed Maryam d'Abo, Kara in *The Living Daylights*. Sat on her sofa she tapped a nail against a photograph of Timothy Dalton and declared "Now *he* was sexy..." In 2012, for Bond's fiftieth anniversary, I commissioned a feature from Christopher Wood, the man who had written *The Spy Who Loved Me*, the film that had so enthralled me in that distant London summer. And each time I went to a press screening of a new Bond film at the Odeon in Leicester Square I felt that distance narrow to nothing.

I've written my own spy thriller novels along the way, The War In The Dark and The Spider Dance. They owe a debt to Bond, naturally, while pushing into even stranger territory, into the realm of the supernatural. I've included a bonus essay on Bond and horror in this book, just to connect the dots.

And then here we are. Mission Statements. It's a celebration, a critique and a history, charting not just the story of the Bond movies but the cultural forces that shaped them.

It's an astonishing thing for a series of films to have lasted for so long. Inevitably they become touchstones for the world beyond them, reflecting our changing tastes and preoccupations as much as they set out to thrill and amuse us. I wanted to contextualise it all.

In the end, of course, it's a personal response. This is me still processing all those glorious adventures swilling in my bloodstream.

An excellent vintage, Mr Bond.

DR. NO

1962 109 minutes

Director: Terence Young

Writers: Richard Maibaum, Johanna Harwood, Berkely Mather

Score: Monty Norman

Title theme: Monty Norman

Cast: Sean Connery, Ursula Andress, Jack Lord, Joseph Wiseman, John Kitzmiller

A NEW AGE

1962, and a bomb-blast of glamour and sophistication is about to hit a Britain still mired in the charcoal gloom of postwar austerity. Yes, this is the year that the flavoured crisp arrives on Blighty's shores... You can only imagine the impact of James Bond's big screen debut in a land where a packet of Cheese and Onion felt like a minor miracle.

Dr. No captures an age trembling on the edge of huge, lasting change, escaping the certainties of empire and poised to embrace the revolution of the '60s. We're at the cusp of the space age – the film opens with a moon rocket launch at Cape Canaveral, and there's a hint of Sputnik or Telstar's sonic otherworldliness in the eerie bleeps that punctuate the title sequence.

There's a dazzling modernity here, from Peter Hunt's urgent, innovative cutting to the jolting violence (a woman is shot in the opening minutes, and there's blood) to the pulse of sexuality that throbs throughout – raffishly, Bond takes the time to bed Sylvia Trench before turning his attention to saving the world.

A new age is here. And its hero is ready.

BOND... JAMES BOND

Bond's introduction amid the smoke-wreathed gaming tables of Les Ambassadeurs is beautifully staged by director Terence Young. At first Connery is concealed from us, a charismatic centre of gravity around which the other casino patrons are orbiting. It's as if the camera itself is wary of Bond, or at least complicit in his world of secrets and shadows.

A card hits the table. We glimpse an elegant tuxedo sleeve, a glossy, coal-black sweep of hair. A hand reaches for a gleaming cigarette case. And then Connery is revealed to us in close-up, all hooded eyes and half-sneer.

A cigarette hangs languidly from his lips. As he lights it he declares his name with an unmistakably saturnine purr: "Bond. James Bond". And Monty Norman's imminently immortal Bond theme kicks in, already ominous with the promise of the legend to come.

THE CONNERY FACTOR

Connery feels so effortlessly iconic as Bond that it's sobering to remember just what a contentious choice he was.

Eternally class-conscious, Ian Fleming initially considered this former barrow boy too coarse and loutish for his fastidious hero ("I'm looking for Commander James Bond, not an overgrown stuntman.."). United Artists, meanwhile, flinched at the thought of an unknown scoring so coveted a role. Terence Young may have preferred to assign 007's licence to kill to Richard Johnson, but he clearly saw the potential in Connery and took it upon himself to sculpt the Scotsman's raw matter.

Young marched Connery to his tailor, clad him in Turnbull & Asser shirts, instructed him to kip in his suit until Bond's immaculate sense of style clung like a second skin. But just enough of Connery's brutish smoulder remained: his 007 would forever feel like a wildcat in gentleman's disguise.

And while Connery's distinctive voice would fuel endless pub impressions his accent was, he claimed, key to his take on Bond. "Because I'm Scottish I stress certain words differently," he told The Guardian in 1971. "The Scots, for instance, say: how are *you*? The English say: how *are* you? I hate the poetry voice. The poetry should speak for itself. Because of my word-stress I was able to get away from the original Bond character and take the sting out of those bad taste jokes that crop up in the films."

JUST SAY NO

"I never fail, Mr Bond," declares the master of Crab Key. With his crisp collarless suit and strangely robotic, black-gloved hands ("A misfortune," he pronounces, with tantalising understatement), the first big screen Bond villain feels like the archetype for every world-grasping madman that follows. He's already part of a long tradition, though, rooted in the Penny Dreadful devilry of such empire-threatening masterminds as Fu Manchu, created by Sax Rohmer in 1913.

Ian Fleming approached Noel Coward for the title role – Coward's response? "Dr No? No! No! No!" – while Christopher Lee declined the chance to take on 007 a whole decade before his turn as Francisco Scaramanga in *The Man With The Golden Gun*. Acclaimed Broadway actor Joseph Wiseman won the part and played No in pseudo-Asian make-up, his face an implacable mannequin mask.

HONEY TO THE B

Ursula Andress arrives an hour into *Dr. No* but it feels as though cinema has been waiting for her forever.

It's one of the screen's most heart-stopping entrances: she emerges from the blue of the Caribbean like some bikini-clad valkyrie or warrior Venus, a sea-shell in her hand and a knife strapped to her shining thigh. You can almost hear the rulebook of celluloid sexuality being torn into tiny pieces. "What are you doing here, looking for shells?" she asks Bond. "No, I'm just looking," he replies, for once the voice of the audience.

The role of Honey Ryder remained uncast as late as two weeks before filming began – the producers offered Andress the part without even a face to face meeting, smitten by some striking photos taken by her husband John Derek. Andress suffered for her immortality: striding from the waves she tore her leg open on some lurking coral. That celebrated image, Bond girl incarnate, actually captures her with a painfully swollen knee.

BOND'S WORLD

Dr. No creates a unique cinemascape for its hero, one poised between the old world and the new. Fleming's beloved Jamaica is here, all colonial privilege, Cotton Island shirts and gentlemanly games of cards beneath a hot, listless sun. Big Ben, meanwhile, stands stately and reassuring in the British night as a secret service radio room fills with the urgent chatter of espionage.

Elsewhere there's a thrilling futurism: production designer Ken Adam spent $100,000 on the movie's centrepiece nuclear control room set, conjuring a multi-tiered dream of atomic age tech. But Adam's genius didn't always require serious bankrolling: one of the movie's most memorable sets is simply a marble floor, some cunningly deployed shadows and a spider in a cage. It's a masterclass in minimalist menace.

INTERCEPTED INTELLIGENCE

Filming began on January 16th 1962. The first scene to be shot was Bond strolling past the photographer in the airport.

Ian Fleming was so impressed with the film's leading lady that he slipped a mention of Ursula Andress into On Her Majesty's Secret Service.

Andress's appearance created a huge spike in global bikini sales.

Dr. No sees the first appearance of the character who would later become known as Q. Peter Burton plays Major Boothroyd, the MI6 armourer who equips Bond with his signature Walther.

It was Ben Fish, a friend of producer Harry Saltzman, who suggested Connery for the role of 007.

FROM RUSSIA WITH LOVE

1963 115 minutes

Director: Terence Young

Writers: Richard Maibaum, Johanna Harwood, Berkely Mather

Score: John Barry

Title song: Matt Munro

Cast: Sean Connery, Daniela Bianchi, Robert Shaw, Lotte Lenya, Pedro Armendáriz

EAST BY NORTH EAST

Armed with twice the money of *Dr. No*, *From Russia With Love* emerges as a handsome, well–tailored espionage tale, one that sees Bond stride towards true global phenomenon status.

Life magazine had recently revealed that Fleming's original novel was one of John F Kennedy's favourite reads, and the endorsement of the free world's ultimate alpha male bestowed the kind of heat that no publicity budget could buy.

While *Dr. No* flirted with an atomic age sense of the fantastic, this sleek Cold War caper feels in thrall to Alfred Hitchcock, Hollywood's sly, portly monarch of suspense. The Lector machine is a perfect Hitchcockian MacGuffin while leading lady Daniela Bianchi is the kind of glacially immaculate blonde that sparked the director's darkest fantasies. 1959's *North By North West* is the clear inspiration here, from the cross-country romance and intrigue of the train journey to the sequence where Bond is hounded by a low-flying helicopter, just like Cary Grant being buzzed by a pernicious cropduster. Hitchcock was wooed to direct a Bond in the earliest days of the franchise, but that's one potential masterpiece the film gods cruelly denied us.

WORLDS WITHIN WORLDS

From Russia With Love is the Bond saga's definitive spy story, and its landscape is a mirror-maze of deception and illusion.

Istanbul feels like an ever-shifting puzzle box in the eternal war of nerves between East and West, its dark, haunted alleyways and decaying buildings masking all manner of chicanery. Bond's ally Kerim Bey takes him on a boat ride through the secret, flooded city beneath its streets, where rats throng in the shadows and a crafty periscope peers into the Russian consulate.

Elsewhere a giant movie poster on the side of a house hides its own secrets, the oversized smile of a starlet transforming into a private escape hatch for enemy agents. Hotel rooms are infested with listening devices, mirrors conceal the whirring gaze of cameras, a humble attache case is a deadly arsenal, SMERSH is really SPECTRE and even the lovely Tatiana is a honeytrap, a ruse to ensnare Her Majesty's secret servant. Trust no one, Mr Bond…

"A NASTY LITTLE CHRISTMAS PRESENT"

Technically, Bond's Q Branch briefcase isn't the first gadget we see him use – he has a geiger counter in *Dr. No* and uses a then thrillingly futuristic pager and car phone in his introductory scene in this film. But it's the first true gadget as we know it, where an everyday object is loaded with some cunningly lethal modifications and emerges as the kind of hardware a vicious but imaginative schoolboy might blueprint.

Disguised as "An ordinary black leather case", it conceals 20 rounds of ammunition, a flat throwing knife, an AR7 folding sniper's rifle with infra-red sight, 50 gold sovereigns and a talcum powder tin stocked with tear gas. Its latches, naturally, are booby-trapped. Desmond Llewellyn makes his debut as Q, MI6's resident tweedy tech-head, and in years to come the scenes where he gifts the gadgets to a wryly amused 007 would become a beloved part of the Bond ritual.

THE TRAIN FIGHT

The brawl between Bond and Red Grant on the Orient Express is one of the tensest, most adrenalised fight scenes in cinema. What makes it so effective is that it's a battle of equals – "We're pros, Mr Bond," says the SMERSH hitman, clearly as coldly proficient a killer as MI6's finest. But it's a sequence spiced with a seething undercurrent of rivalry and just a twist of psychosexual weirdness.

Facing Bond, Grant radiates disdain and envy – his choice of red wine with fish has just exposed him as a sham sophisticate – and he orders 007 to "Crawl over here and kiss my foot." And then a bullet takes out a light, a train window shatters and the two besuited bruisers crash between the carriages in a choking swirl of tear gas. There's no music, just the sound of fists on flesh, the rattle and the gallop of the train wheels, the evil whisper of Grant's garroting wire. Bond stabs him in the arm and then, finally, throttles him with his own weapon, a death that feels rewarding, hard-earned.

Adjusting his tie, our hero's face is a mask of sweat. For once there's no blackly comic quip, just a dismissive snarl of "Old man," Grant's own snide catchphrase. Shot with three cameras in a confined space, stuntmen only employed for one shot, it's a brutal, bruising masterclass in screen combat.

FROM RUSSIA WITH KINK

For its time, this is an astonishingly sexy movie. Take the title sequence. We're still a long way from the provocative silhouettes of later Bond films, but there's a genuine erotic shimmer as credits are projected on the bodies of glittering, bejewelled belly dancers. It's a lo-fi solution by titles designer Robert Brownjohn that conjures a sultry burlesque vibe.

Elsewhere two flashing-eyed gypsy girls fight to the death, all claws and cleavage. Bond actually stops the bout – and takes both of them to bed, still the only cheeky threesome in the franchise's long history of sauce. There's a perverse tingle, too, in the scene where Rosa Klebb places her hand on Tatiana's knee. "You are a fine looking girl," declares the SPECTRE gorgon, as the innocent cypher clerk flinches.

Tatiana's seduction scene with Bond deploys one of the most outrageous double entendres in Bond history: "I think my mouth's too big," she frets. "No, it's the right size," Bond reassures her. "For me, that is." The fact that SPECTRE agents are secretly filming their romp through a two-way mirror only adds to the frisson of kink.

THE SPECTRES AT THE FEAST

While *Dr. No* found Bond facing a single threat in Crab Key's cold-eyed mastermind, *From Russia With Love* fields no less than three villains. Vladek Sheybal is Kronsteen, SPECTRE's reptillian chess master, while Robert Shaw earned one of the defining roles of his career as Donald "Red" Grant, a convicted murderer and Dartmoor escapee ("Homicidal paranoiac – superb material..."). A physical match for Connery, the black-gloved Grant is a cool, watchful presence for the majority of the film, forever in the shadows – unseen, he even quietly saves Bond's life at one point.

But the most memorable player in this fiendish troika is Lotte Lenya as Rosa Klebb, a Russian defector in poison-spiked shoes. Lenya may have played Klebb as a frump, all bottle-glasses and prison warden hair, but in one of the great, forgotten ironies she first found fame as a glamorous cabaret star in her native Germany.

INTERCEPTED INTELLIGENCE

We see the tentacled-skull SPECTRE symbol for the first time in this film – it's a note on the bottom of a glass, summoning Kronsteen.

It's also our first glimpse of Blofeld, SPECTRE's enigmatic Number One, though this incarnation has a whole head of glossy black hair.

Blofeld's hands belong to Anthony Dawson from *Dr. No*, who also did screentests with potential Bond girls. The voice is Eric Pohlman.

The billboard escape hatch advertises *Call Me Bwana*, another Broccoli/Saltzman production. The star is Anita Ekberg (Marilyn Monroe in Fleming's novel).

SPECTRE replaced SMERSH as the principal threat to avoid upsetting the USSR.

Daniela Bianchi also appeared in 1967 Bond spoof *Operation Kid Brother*, alongside Sean's true-life sibling Neil.

Peter Burton was unavailable to reprise the role of Boothroyd, so Desmond Llewellyn won the role of MI6's "equipment officer" instead.

GOLDFINGER

1964 110 minutes

Director: Guy Hamilton

Writers: Richard Maibaum, Paul Dehn, Johanna Harwood, Berkely Mather

Score: John Barry

Title song: Shirley Bassey

Cast: Sean Connery, Honor Blackman, Gert Fröbe, Tania Mallet, Harold Sakata

THE GOLD STANDARD

"It's another Bondbuster!" bragged the marketing - but, arguably, *Goldfinger* was the first, the film whose blend of carnival thrills, outsized ambition and cheeky wit defined not just the notion of a Bond movie but every quip-studded action flick that followed.

Guy Hamilton replaced Terence Young as director, substituting a quicksilver energy and lightness of touch for his predecessor's old world panache. It's a film with a matchless swagger, energised by the growing power of the Bond brand. Just watch as the camera swoops low into Miami, John Barry's score sounding impossibly bullish as we sail past a parade of poolside beauties – soon one of the defining cliches of the franchise – and the promise of good times under the Florida sun.

It feels a world away from *Dr. No*'s superstition-haunted Caribbean or *From Russia With Love*'s intrigue-soaked Istanbul, but this brash American landscape of empty highways, vast horizons and drive-in diners must have seemed just as exotic to British moviegoers of the early '60s.

A wry sense of absurdity infiltrates the series for the first time: Bond's underwater mission in the pre-titles finds him with a duck disguise on his head. Connery rips it off with the same ill-concealed contempt he reportedly reserved for removing his toupee after a take.

HE LOVES ONLY GOLD

Goldfinger not only sets the house style of the Bond movies – it gives us the first bona fide Bond song too (the titles of *Dr. No* and *From Russia With Love* had played over instrumental versions of their themes, though a snatch of a crooning Matt Monro drifts from a transistor radio in the latter).

As sold by Shirley Bassey in imperious, full-throated diva mode, it's an incorrigible tart of a show tune, all brass stabs, pomp and menace. The words "Pretty girl, beware" feel like a foreshadowing – Bond leaves a trail of death behind him in this film, with both Masterson sisters losing their lives in memorably nasty ways.

Robert Brownjohn designed the film's innovative title sequence, which mixes eerie surrealism (the Aston Martin's tumbling numberplates replace the mouth of a girl – Dali would have approved) and brazen, molten eroticism, as flames lick the thighs of a golden girl. It's all very sexy, aloof and sinister and feels deeply, brilliantly Bond.

ALL THAT GLITTERS

"Man has climbed Mount Everest, gone to the bottom of the ocean," declares karat-lusting rascal Auric Goldfinger. "He has fired rockets at the moon, split the atom, achieved miracles in every field of human endeavour… except crime!"

Take one look at Ken Adam's phenomenal Fort Knox set, gaze at its gleaming walkways and impossible mountains of bullion, and just for a moment you share Goldfinger's insane ambition.

Originally the setpiece climax was to take place at the gates of America's high security gold reserve. An instinctive showman, Cubby Broccoli knew that the audience needed more. "I want to see a cathedral of gold," he demanded, dreaming big, and Adam delivered, his ignorance of the building's real interior forcing him to concoct a glittering fantasy treasure house that leaves the reality for dead.

ODDJOB MAN

Goldfinger's golfball-crushing manservant establishes another mainstay of big screen Bond lore – the freaky henchman with the lethal twist. As Oddjob, Harold Sakata is a silent, smiling, impeccably mannered tub of muscle, forever shadowed by an eerie tinkling on the soundtrack. Dapper and malevolent, he's the angel of death after a stint in butler school.

Sakata won a silver medal for weightlifting at the 1948 Olympics and was spotted by Guy Hamilton while wrestling on TV under the name Tosh Togo. *Goldfinger* was his first break in acting, and he came to it with admirable professionalism. He was badly burned during the electrocution scene on the Fort Knox set, refusing to let go of the sparking wire until he heard Hamilton say "Cut!"

PUSSY POWER

A recently concussed Bond returns to consciousness. A haughty but twinkly blonde swims into focus before his eyes. "My name is Pussy Galore," she announces. Bond smirks, visibly swallows. "I must be dreaming," he murmurs. Watch this scene in the 21st Century and you might be baffled by the long silence that follows, a strange blank space in the scene that makes perfect sense once you realise it's built-in recovery time for the original audience to stop laughing.

Yes, it's one of the screen's filthiest double entendres – fretful studio execs even considered neutering the name to Kitty Galore – and it's to Honor Blackman's credit that Goldfinger's personal pilot is remembered as so much more than just a shameless piece of wordplay.

Blackman was a household name already thanks to her turn as dominatrix daredevil Cathy Gale in *The Avengers*, and she brings to Pussy all the charm, steel and self-possession of one of John Steed's partners. She was used to doing her judo moves on the unforgiving concrete floor of a TV studio, so her scrap in the hay with Sean Connery felt like a luxury.

THE CAR'S THE STAR

An elegant silver bullet, enshrined forever in Corgi toy form, Bond's tricked-out DB5 remains 007's definitive set of wheels (he drives a stately 1933 Bentley convertible in the Fleming books).

The management at Aston Martin needed some persuading at first. Was this really the kind of thing they wanted their prestigious marque to be associated with? Finally they relented and loaned the filmmakers the prototype of their desirable new baby, still sceptical that the film's effects technicians could squeeze any more gizmology into its chassis.

On *Goldfinger*'s release the car became a phenomenon, arguably eclipsing Connery himself. Its introduction also gives us our first Q lab scene, soon to be a mainstay of the franchise. Connery's sardonic incredulity sells it, of course - "Ejector seat? You're joking!" – but so does Desmond Llewellyn's deadpan self-belief in the glorious absurdity of it all. "I never joke about my work, 007!"

THE GOLDEN GIRL

It's the imperishable image of the film – Shirley Eaton's gilded corpse, laid on a hotel bed. And it sums up the essential DNA of the Bond films in a single, potent visual. It's as elegant as it's sinister, as sexy as it's menacing, as poisonous as it's alluring.

Just watch Connery's war of emotions as he discovers Jill's gold-painted body. His face shifts from genuinely startled to professionally intrigued to, finally, a fleeting sadness at the realisation that Jill is the latest piece of collateral damage in his deadly lifestyle.

"It didn't occur to me that I was naked," said Shirley Eaton, who graced the cover of Life magazine in November 1964, a vision of 24 karat glamour.

INTERCEPTED INTELLIGENCE

While Shirley Eaton is the gold-plated victim on screen, *Carry On* starlet Margaret Nolan is the golden girl in the title sequence and posters (Nolan also appears as Dink in this movie).

My Fair Lady's Theodore Bikel nearly won the role of Goldfinger.

Goldfinger's laser is the first time such a device had been seen on screen.

Guy Hamilton's hassle with parking tickets in London inspired the idea of the Aston's revolving numberplates.

Hamilton told Desmond Llewellyn that Q must never admire Bond, even though Llewellyn's instinct was to stand when his superior officer entered the room.

There's a nod to Goldfinger in the 1965 *Avengers* episode "Too Many Christmas Trees", where Steed receives a card from Cathy Gale and wonders whatever she can be doing at Fort Knox…

THUNDERBALL

1965 130 minutes

Director: Terence Young

Writers: Richard Maibaum, John Hopkins, Jack Whittingham, Kevin McClory

Score: John Barry

Title song: Tom Jones

Cast: Sean Connery, Claudine Auger, Adolfo Celi, Luciana Paluzzi, Rik Van Nutter

HERE COMES THE BIGGEST BOND OF ALL!

As ambitious as the SPECTRE scheme that propels it, *Thunderball* is the moment the Bond franchise finally embraces its own phenomenon.

By 1965 pop culture was inescapably spy-crazed. While *Thunderball*'s $5.6 million budget may seem small beer in comparison to Blofeld's $100 million ransom demand, it armed 007 against the legion of low-grade imitators coveting his licence to kill at the box office. From its first moments it's a tale that trades in widescreen wow: the jet-pack in the pre-titles makes Bond a science fiction rocketman and leaves his waiting

Aston Martin looking rather mundane. Elsewhere the heist of the Vulcan bombers is accomplished with a genuine sense of scale, their stolen nuclear payloads perverting what Harold Wilson called "the white heat of technology" into something monstrous and deadly.

There's a case to be made for *Thunderball* as the first true techno-thriller. Its fetishised military firepower has all the gunmetal gleam of a Tom Clancy novel.

SPECTRAL ACTIVITY

Blofeld remains faceless in *Thunderball*, a dapper, cat-stroking presence whose voice is an unplaceable purr. But amid a strikingly modernist Ken Adam set we finally glimpse the heart of his organisation.

Amusingly, for all its world-threatening stratagems and casual disdain for human life, SPECTRE is clearly mired in file-shuffling bureaucracy. There are financial briefings, departmental reports about consultation fees and casual mention of an execution branch. It is, frankly, local council hell. The electrified chairs only add to the satirical bite.

Of course there's a camp joy in an ultra-secret cabal whose members are easily identified by a distinctive octopus ring. But perhaps there's something darker, more interesting here. SPECTRE's multi-tentacled avatar has a Lovecraftian shiver, after all, recalling the cosmic horror of Cthulu. Watch as Largo kisses the ring after throwing an underling into a shark-filled pool. It's a moment that carries the subliminal echo of blood sacrifice, as if SPECTRE's Number Two is making an offering to an ancient, soul-hungering god...

WE NEED TO TALK ABOUT KEVIN

Another, altogether different spectre looms over *Thunderball*, one that would shadow the Bond saga for decades.

Ian Fleming always itched to see his hero enshrined on celluloid and, in 1958, he teamed with writer/director Kevin McClory and veteran screenwriter Jack Whittingham on a film provisionally titled *James Bond Of The Secret Service* (also known variously as *SPECTRE* and, more evocatively, *Longitude 78 West*).

Fleming cheekily recycled the core elements of this nuclear kidnap caper as his 1961 novel Thunderball, a move that outraged his collaborators and prompted a high profile legal case that left the author with the rights to the book but granted McClory cinematic ownership of the story.

When Bond producers Broccoli and Saltzman came to film Thunderball they enlisted McClory as producer, a pragmatic pact that brought a potential rival on side. But McClory was a timebomb. A decade later he began preparations to mount his own Bond movie, *Warhead* – a loose remake of *Thunderball* bolstered by the star power of Sean Connery, no less – and his claims to the creation of Blofeld and SPECTRE would see these key elements purged from the official Bond franchise.

McClory finally remade *Thunderball* as 1983's *Never Say Never Again*, complete with a fiftysomething Connery. In the late '90s he was still threatening to launch his own, competing Bond franchise, doubtlessly recombining the narrative DNA of Thunderball in infinite combinations…

HE KNOWS THE MEANING OF SUCCESS

The Aston Martin's aqua-jets flood the screen. Sea nymphs emerge, graceful, naked, their hair trailing in ocean currents, inky silhouettes against blood red water, pursued by the unmistakably phallic threat of harpoons. It's the first archetypal Bond title sequence, loaded with the weaponised sexuality that would come to define the work of Maurice Binder, the designer of each flashy, fleshy intro until 1989's *Licence To Kill*.

The title song itself sees *Goldfinger*'s assurance edge perilously close to bombast. "Every woman he wants he will get," belts out Tom Jones, possibly singing from the heart of his own little black book. "His days of asking are all gone." After Shirley Bassey's lauding of Auric Goldfinger as the man with the Midas touch it's natural to see this as an equally ominous celebration of Emilio Largo, *Thunderball*'s main villain. But what if Bond is "the winner who takes it all"? It's tempting to see this song as a hymn to 007 himself, now revelling in his status as king of pop culture.

John Barry's incidental music, meanwhile, is mesmeric and serpentine, the perfect soundtrack to the shifting realities and hidden machinations of Bond's world.

SEA FEVER

Knowing that an entire quarter of *Thunderball*'s screentime needed to take place underwater, Broccoli summoned Ivan Tors Films, specialists in such sub-aquatic screen fare as *Flipper*. The film is enhanced no end by their expertise – a throwaway scene where Domino rides a turtle through forests of coral and darting fish is captured with impeccable clarity, a rare moment of genuine beauty for a Bond flick.

The climactic skirmish between SPECTRE and the forces of the West provided the biggest challenge, requiring weeks of rehearsal and the precise choreography of some 60 divers who could only communicate via hand signals. Many argue that *Thunderball*'s final reel combat sequence is a slog, an interminable tussle between faceless, voiceless opponents, but there's an eerie grandeur to this undersea battle, punctuated with truly arresting imagery. Storms of blood fill the water as the sharks move in, a random crab scuttles monstrously in the middle of the fight and Largo's lone, glaring eye fills his visor with Cyclopean hate…

SHARK! SHARK!

"Magnificent creatures," declares Largo, with the pride of a true supervillain in his man-eating pets. "The notorious Golden Grotto sharks. The most savage, the most dangerous. They know when it's time to be fed…"

Sharks are part of the core iconography of the Bond movies. They also lend a darkly-gliding menace to *Live And Let Die*, *The Spy Who Loved Me* and *Licence To Kill*. But our hero's closest encounter with them comes in *Thunderball*. For the scene where Bond infiltrates the shark pool, production designer Ken Adam procured 15 of the beasts from a Miami aquarium. Connery was naturally reluctant to share the water with these carnivorous co-stars, but director Terence Young assured him that there would be a plexiglass corridor separating him from the creatures: "Only way they can get in is if they jump like a dolphin." "How do I know sharks can't do that?" retorted Connery.

What Young neglected to tell his star was that there would be a crucial four foot gap in the defence as Adam hadn't been able to locate enough plexiglass. Watch Bond's pop-eyed reaction to the entrance of the shark – that's not acting. A shaken, furious Connery fled the pool seconds later.

INTERCEPTED INTELLIGENCE

Broccoli and Saltzman originally eyed Thunderball as their first Bond adaptation, but the legal situation over the screen rights deterred them.

The movie's original theme song was Mr Kiss Kiss Bang Bang, recorded by both Shirley Bassey and Dionne Warwick. The producers exchanged it for a number that foregrounded the film's title, but ghost traces of it remain in Barry's score.

The sharks in the underwater battle were controlled by a system of wires through their fins.

Director Terence Young's wife refused to sleep with him for two weeks because she insisted he stank of shark.

The Operation Thunderball file has the words On Her Majesty's Secret Service stamped on it.

Julie Christie, Raquel Welch and Faye Dunaway were all in consideration for the role of Domino.

Tom Jones fainted in the recording booth while attempting to hold the final note of Thunderball (listen closely and you might just hear a big Welsh thump…)

YOU ONLY LIVE TWICE

1967 117 minutes

Director: Lewis Gilbert

Writers: Roald Dahl, Harold Jack Bloom

Score: John Barry

Title song: Nancy Sinatra

Cast: Sean Connery, Akiko Wakabayashi, Mie Hama, Donald Pleasence, Karin Dor

TWICE IS THE ONLY WAY TO LIVE

Fittingly for a film that opens in Earth orbit, this is the moment big screen Bond first escapes the gravitational force of Fleming's novels.

Originally published in 1964, You Only Live Twice was a strange, fatalistic tale, a collision of pulp and poetry saturated with the imagery of death (little wonder – Fleming wrote it while recovering from the first of the heart attacks that would ultimately claim him). More fairytale than thriller, it found Blofeld stalking an ancient Japanese castle in a suit of Samurai armour, tending a nightmarish Garden of Death whose poisonous horticulture lures the young and suicidal.

The filmmakers retained the book's Japanese backdrop but, fearing the box office gamble of straying too far from their killer formula, chose to craft their own story, opting for space age spectacle and traditional spy-flick kicks in place of Fleming's high weirdness.

To pen the film they hired Roald Dahl – an unproven screenwriter, but a friend of Fleming's and a man whose mordant, macabre short stories showed the mix of wit and kinkiness the Bond films demanded. But just a hint of folklore remains among the ultramodern thrills: there's a forbidden cave, a disfigured demon who hides beneath a metal lake and a kiss on a secret mountain where the sky itself kills the unwary. Elsewhere, beads of poison drip down a wire like deadly pearls into the mouth of a sleeping girl; the moment feels torn from an especially dark fairytale.

"BAD NEWS FROM OUTER SPACE!"

There's a simple, matchless excitement in the white circle that prowls the screen in the opening frames of any Bond film. It arrives loaded with promise and possibility. We wait for its enticing blankness to fill with our first glimpse of some new and exotic locale, some tantalising hint of the caper to come.

This time it offers a breathtaking leap: an image of a space capsule among the stars, the blue curve of the Earth below. *Dr. No* may have dabbled in mad scientist sci-fi, and *Thunderball* may have strapped a jet-pack to 007's back, but this is a startling new frontier for Bond. It's a topical choice of arena, though – in 1967 the world's superpowers were locked in a race for the Moon, the Apollo landing a long two years away. There was a real sense that the true Cold War was taking place far above the planet. Bond himself would only leave Earth's orbit in 1979's *Star Wars*-chasing *Moonraker*, but the silent, remote battleground of outer space is where the true stakes play out in *You Only Live Twice*. The sight of SPECTRE's alligator-jawed spacecraft, its maw opening like an evil steel bloom, is one of the most haunting visuals in the Bond canon.

"EXTORTION IS MY BUSINESS!"

You Only Live Twice is the movie that finally unmasks Blofeld. Not too quickly, though. Until his final confrontation with 007 he remains a collection of sinister cues: a beige-jacketed arm, an octopus-emblazoned ring, the immortal white cat.

"Allow me to introduce myself," he declares, his voice loaded with exquisite menace. "I am Ernst Stavro Blofeld." And there's Donald Pleasence, looking like a scarred egg, his face positively melted with evil. A man with the private piranha pool of a truly well-appointed supervillain, his crazed half-shriek of "Kill Bond! Now" is rather hard to square with the calm bureaucrat of *Thunderball* and *From Russia With Love*.

Pleasence was, in fact, a replacement Blofeld. Czech actor Jan Werich was originally signed to play the SPECTRE mastermind but was dismissed after five days of filming for not being sufficiently sinister. "He looked like a rather benevolent Father Christmas," recalled director Lewis Gilbert.

FLIGHT AND FIGHT

"Oh, she's a wonderful girl… quite small, very fast!" Taking to the Japanese skies like some rocket-loaded wasp, Q's gift of Little Nellie is one of the more unlikely but most beloved vehicles in Bond history. And Bond clearly loves her too: for once he listens to the gadget-master's instructions without his usual bass note of mockery (though naturally he can't resist buzzing Q after lift-off).

There's a cute sense of functionality to this personal gyro-copter and, as we see it assembled before our eyes from parts in crates, an unmistakable whiff of the Great British Shed about it, too.

In real life it was the creation of Wing Commander Ken Wallis, war veteran and inventor. Production designer Ken Adam heard Wallis talking about the craft on the radio and, sensing a potential crowdpleaser, phoned the BBC to be put in touch. Adam reimagined the single-seater autogyro as a compact "war machine", armed with flamethrower, blazing machine-guns and air-to-air missiles - a handy arsenal for engaging SPECTRE in hostile airspace.

UNDER THE VOLCANO

Concealed below a sliding lake, Blofeld's volcanic headquarters is the definitive supervillain lair: a secret underground nest buzzing with boilersuited paramilitary activity and the thrum of monorails.

"I knew if it didn't work I would never work in movies again," remembered Ken Adam, who asked for $1 million to construct the movie's centrepiece set. It was a budget-bruising sum in 1967, more than the entire cost of *Dr. No*. Broccoli didn't even blink.

So ambitious was the undertaking (it even boasted its own working heli-pad) that the crew of plasterers and riggers demanded danger money for the towering set's construction. Once completed, cinematographer Freddie Young requisitioned every last lamp in Pinewood Studios to actually light the gargantuan stage. With its monstrous air of grim, industrial menace, this showpiece set was proof that the once modest

Bond movies were now dreaming bigger and bolder than anyone else in cinema. The world was not enough…

TURNING JAPANESE

Matched to the dreaming strings of John Barry's most romantic score yet, the Japanese location lends a welcome exotica to *You Only Live Twice*. Fleming was not only a thriller writer – he was an accomplished travel journalist too, and he brings that sharp, inquisitive eye to many of his Bond tales. This movie has a little of that travelogue shimmer.

Tokyo itself is a thrilling collision of old and new. Neon signs and impatient car horns mix with rickshaws and bicycle bells, while Bond strolls confidently through the dazzling chaos in a sharp suit, the unshakable international traveller, 20th Century man incarnate.

The bright white gleam of Aki's gadget-laden Toyota– yes, for once the Bond girl has the wheels, and earns the Corgi toy – makes an effective contrast to the shadowy cool of Tiger Tanaka's ninja force, the first appearance of the ninja in Western pop culture ("The art of concealment and surprise, Bond-san!"). Best not to dwell on Connery's undercover makeover from hulking Scotsman to Japanese fisherman. Is that a Beatle wig?

INTERCEPTED INTELLIGENCE

The producers originally intended to make *On Her Majesty's Secret Service* before *You Only Live Twice*.

Toho Studios – creators of the Godzilla films – supplied soundstages, crew and female stars.

Production designer Ken Adam spent three weeks scouring two thirds of Japan, flying seven hours a day, hunting for the perfect location for Blofeld's base.

The true life ninjas hired for the climax turned out not to like heights – they baulked at the idea of descending on ropes from the roof of the 148 ft tall set.

The Little Nellie sequence was actually completed in Spain. Japan didn't want rockets fired over one of their national parks.

This is the first time that we see Fleming's hero in full naval uniform – a reminder that he's Commander Bond (Royal Navy Reserve).

Before Nancy Sinatra recorded *You Only Live Twice*, Julie Rogers sang a very different, ultimately discarded title song.

ON HER MAJESTY'S SECRET SERVICE

1969 142 minutes

Director: Peter Hunt

Writers: Richard Maibaum, Simon Raven

Score: John Barry

Title theme: John Barry

Cast: George Lazenby, Diana Rigg, Telly Savalas, Ilse Steppat, Gabriele Ferzetti

THE IMPROBABLE BOND

Imagine an alternate 1960s where Paul McCartney bails on the Beatles on the eve of *Sgt Pepper*. His replacement? An Australian busker who's never written a song in his life. In our universe much the same sense of seismic improbability accompanied George Lazenby's appointment as the cinema's second James Bond.

Connery had declared his intention to quit as he flew East to film *You Only Live Twice*, resentful of the Faustian trade-off between international stardom and his private life (his arrival in Japan triggered mob scenes that necessitated bodyguards and police blockades, and even found the press hounding him into the gents).

Broccoli and Saltzman briefly considered reinventing 007 as a hip, contemporary anti-hero attuned to the counter-culture but realised that what the franchise really needed was "another Sean Connery". Enter George Lazenby, an Australian male model whose brand of cheery hunkster charm was most famously showcased in a commercial for Big Fry chocolate.

Lazenby knew his limitations as an actor – "I hadn't even spoken in front of cameras" – but his agent convinced him he had the requisite arrogance for Fleming's hero. Lazenby chased the gig with a crafty, laser-sighted tenacity, purchasing one of Connery's cast-off suits from his tailor and having his hair cut by the Scotsman's regular barber at the Dorchester.

"I've got to level with you," he told the producers. "I'm not an actor." Broccoli and Saltzman refused to be fazed, confident in their starmaking power. When Lazenby broke the nose of a Russian wrestler in a screen test it was the moment that won him the coveted licence to kill. "I'm really looking forward to being Bond," he told Life, "for the bread and the birds."

BY GEORGE

To many Lazenby is the critical faultline in *On Her Majesty's Secret Service*, an otherwise immaculately crafted adaptation of Fleming's 1963 novel. And, in a sense, he's a fatal piece of miscasting – a raw, untested performer pitched into the most emotionally demanding tale in the Bond canon. But for all his inexperience he brings some genuinely intriguing new colours to 007.

"The new Bond," championed the trailer. "The different Bond." While his introduction echoes Connery's reveal in *Dr. No* – a half-glimpsed man places a cigarette to his lips and lets a lighter spark as the Bond theme stirs – he quickly proves a very different proposition to his predecessor. "Good morning!" he tells a freshly rescued Tracy, on a dawn-lit Portuguese beach. "My name's Bond... James Bond!" There's no hint of Connery's predatory snarl, just a good-natured delight in speaking those famous words.

For all his brawling physicality there's a winning boyishness to Lazenby's Bond, although he feels like an impetuous junior clerk in his scenes with M, and the moment where he appropriates the centrefold from a copy of Playboy is, let's be honest, more schoolboy than true international lounge lizard.

Above all, he's a newly vulnerable Bond. At the winter carnival he's startled like a child by the sudden sight of a man in a polar bear costume. Stripped of his habitual arsenal of gadgetry (there's no traditional Q scene) he's forced to rely on his wits, ripping the pockets from his trousers to create makeshift gloves to inch along a cable car line. It's this vulnerability, along with an unsuspected sweet, chivalric side, that sells the idea of Bond falling in love. Just look at the scene where Bond proposes to Tracy in the snowbound stable. "I love you," confesses the man who never falls in love. "I know I'll never find another girl like you. Will you marry me?" Lazenby's untutored charm perfectly captures the tenderness of the moment, the assailable heart behind the licence to kill.

THE OTHER FELLA

On Her Majesty's Secret Service is a film in fear of the future. All too aware of Connery's absence it wraps his replacement in the armour of nostalgia.

Tellingly, the clock hands in the title sequence sweep backwards, the franchise unspooling to show us flashbacks to *Dr. No*, *From Russia With Love*, *Goldfinger*, *Thunderball*, *You Only Live Twice…* frames of the past quite at odds with the urgent, onward surge of John Barry's propulsively modern theme. We may have all the time in the world, but that time clearly belongs to Sean Connery.

One early scene finds Bond rifling through souvenirs of past missions; we see Honey's knife, Red Grant's watch, the breathing device from *Thunderball*, each talismanic object

51

accompanied by an appropriately evocative musical cue. Elsewhere a janitor whistles the theme to *Goldfinger*. Lazenby simply isn't allowed to escape the shadow of his precursor.

There's no explanation for Bond's change of face (and, four Bonds later, we know that none is needed) but the dialogue acknowledges it with a wink: "Same old James," declares Moneypenny. "Only more so!" It's Lazenby himself who delivers the slyest line, a beat before the titles kick in: "This never happened to the other fella!" A shockingly direct bullet fired into the fourth wall, it's an even more mischievous and knowing moment than Connery was ever allowed.

BEYOND THE ICE

Director Peter Hunt demanded one thing from *On Her Majesty's Secret Service* – reality. So it's a film that trades the soundstage fantasias of previous Bonds for the real world. Blofeld's mountain-crowning eyrie was actually Piz Gloria, a true life restaurant perched on the Schilthorn near Murren in Switzerland (the filmmakers actually constructed the working helipad the screenplay required).

The location saw the first ski-chase sequence in the Bond films and such snow-slicing action would soon become one of the franchise's definitive traditions, reoccurring in *The Spy Who Loved Me*, *For Your Eyes Only*, *A View To A Kill* and

The World Is Not Enough. The Alps themselves are a constant, majestic presence in *OHMSS*, from the snow-swathed night-blue slopes that backdrop Bond's escape from the SPECTRE lair to the blood-hued skies that accompany the stunning final chopper assault. It's a movie that convinces you that you're breathing blade-sharp alpine air.

"MERRY CHRISTMAS, 007!"

Future *Kojak* star Telly Savalas gives us yet another incarnation of Ernst Stavro Blofeld, by now established as Bond's go-to nemesis. This one's a suave, charming thug with a hint of social climber about him. Threatening to unleash an epidemic of sterility through his hypnotised harem of multi-national smashers (perhaps the kitschiest plot yet), his true aim appears to be a full amnesty for past villainy and a recognition of his assumed title as the Count de Bleuchamp.

Savalas brings a newfound physicality to Blofeld (though there's an oddly fey moment when he adjusts the tinsel on a Christmas tree) and in many ways he's a heavy in the mould of *Thunderball*'s Largo, the SPECTRE Number Two. It's notable that far from cat-stroking in the shadows he actually leads the ski pursuit of Bond.

In one of the more baffling lapses in film-to-film continuity Blofeld fails to recognise an undercover Bond, despite meeting him a mere movie before. Or perhaps he does, secretly, know exactly who he is. Perhaps, for both men, the eternal game is a great deal more amusing than the tedious realities of their ongoing battle.

"MR AND MRS JAMES BOND, OF ACACIA AVENUE..."

It's the single most heart-punching moment in the Bond movies: a desolate road, a rake of gunfire, a bullet-hole cobweb-splintering a windscreen, the bloodied face of Bond's new bride, dead, impossibly dead, in his arms.

But Tracy's murder is foreshadowed in the opening moments of *On Her Majesty's Secret Service*. When Bond first sees her it's through a telescopic gun-sight. She's perfectly framed in the cross-hairs, already on borrowed time.

The idea of 007 losing his steel-trap heart to someone was always going to be a hard sell – and the film cheats a little with an incongruous romantic montage of Bond and Tracy strolling with cats and laughing on beaches, like a '60s perfume commercial – but the producers made a smart casting choice in Diana Rigg. Like Honor Blackman before her, she was an alumni of *The Avengers*. If Bond could conceivably marry anyone it would, surely, be Emma Peel (the kids would keep Britain safe for decades).

Ironically there was no love lost between the two leads. "The only time she was cordial was when we had a love scene," recalled Lazenby. "It was an effort for her, but she did try to be nice to me." That reality doesn't begin to intrude on the wrenching final scene, as the agent cradles his dead wife in his arms. He can save the world but he can't save her. He's lost – and he's *lost*. His final sobs are heartbreaking but we're allowed only a moment of grief before the Bond theme kicks in over a shot of bullet-shattered glass. For once the music sounds arrogant, intrusive, bullyingly inevitable. "James Bond 007 will return in *Diamonds Are Forever*" the screen tells us. This game goes on, whatever the cost, however deep the wounds, however lasting the scar tissue.

INTERCEPTED INTELLIGENCE

Other potential replacements for Connery included John Richardson, Anthony Rogers, Robert Campbell and Hans de Vries.

Peter Hunt instructed Lazenby to "Stop that Australian swagger! Walk like Prince Phillip!"

Hunt also encouraged Lazenby to use "This never happened to the other fella" on screen – it had been the Australian's constant refrain during filming.

Lazenby injured his arm while filming a rooftop chase over the streets of London. The scene was cut from the film.

George Baker dubs Lazenby in the scenes where Bond goes undercover as genealogist Sir Hillary Bray. Before Connery's casting Baker was an early candidate for 007 himself.

Lazenby cameoed as 'JB' – at the wheel of a silver Aston Martin – in 1983's TV movie *The Return Of The Man From UNCLE*.

Before We Have All The Time In The World, John Barry's original idea for a love song was The More Things Change, recorded with Nina van Pallandt.

Simon Raven, who supplied additional dialogue, also wrote 1978's BBC TV serial *Sexton Blake And The Demon God*.

Watch the opening gunbarrel sequence again. Lazenby falls to one knee - a subtle nod to the fact that this is the film where Bond proposes...

DIAMONDS ARE FOREVER

1971 120 minutes

Director: Guy Hamilton

Writers: Richard Maibaum, Tom Mankiewicz

Score: John Barry

Title song: Shirley Bassey

Cast: Sean Connery, Jill St John, Charles Gray, Bruce Glover, Putter Smith

NEVER SAY FOREVER AGAIN

Contrary to popular myth, George Lazenby revoked his own licence to kill. He walked from the world of Bond on the advice of Ronan O'Reilly, founder of pirate station Radio Caroline, who persuaded him that there was no place for a government issue assassin in the Age of Aquarius. Fleming's Old Etonian hero was a square, O'Reilly argued, a Saville Row anachronism, relic of a crumbling imperial mindset whose lounge bar refrain of "Vodka martini, shaken not stirred" was positively prehistoric given the prevailing mantra of "Tune in, turn on, drop out."

Lazenby would come to regard this advice as poison in his ear, but for now he was content to holster his Walther PPK, a decision that would ultimately see him trade international stardom for everlasting status as a piece of pub trivia ("The truth of the matter is I was a dumb shit," he later confessed).

Faced with another 007-shaped vacuum, the producers briefly considered enlisting *Batman* star Adam West before signing a fellow American, John Gavin, best known for Hitchcock's *Psycho* and a suave, Bond-like turn in Euro-spy caper *OSS 117 Murder For Sale*. But paymasters United Artists demanded the return of the dependably bankable Sean Connery, and *Dr. No*'s Ursula Andress was despatched to make an offer in person.

Still bruised by the remorseless, privacy-devouring grind of his five film run, Connery mulled the notion for a week, finally accepting a fee of $1 ¼ million that he donated to the Scottish International Education Trust. John Gavin departed, his contract paid in full, his improbably transatlantic Bond doomed to play the picturehouses of a parallel universe. "You've been on holiday," Sir Donald notes as Bond is briefed on his latest mission, the slyest acknowledgement of Connery's return to a role that must have seemed increasingly inescapable.

"WHERE'S BLOFELD?"

It's tempting to see the pre-titles of *Diamonds Are Forever* as a vengeance-fuelled addendum to the climax of *On Her Majesty's Secret Service*. Bond is engaged in a relentless pursuit of Blofeld; an unseen, unflagging force of nature punching, kicking and smashing his way across the planet.

Teasingly withheld for a long minute, Connery's face is finally revealed as he delivers his signature line – "My name's Bond... James Bond!" – and we barely clock his visibly older, more saturnine appearance before he whips a bikini top from a woman and proceeds to strangle her with it.

It's an uncharacteristically malicious moment for a Bond movie and part of a vicious new tone that permeates this entire sequence. 007's jacket pocket conceals a mouse-trap style device that trades Q's usual wit for straightforward cruelty, while Bond slings surgical scalpels with deadly precision, turning SPECTRE goons into shish kebab. Is this savage and merciless new Bond a reaction to Tracy's murder? Tellingly, there's not a single mention of his status as a widower – in fact Moneypenny will later make a joke about wedding rings that would seem to be in deplorable taste – and for all the grim satisfaction of Bond's "Welcome to Hell, Blofeld" as his nemesis sinks into a molten grave, this may as well be a straight sequel to *You Only Live Twice*. Business as usual, Mr Bond.

NEW DECADE, NEW STYLE

Bond targeted the 1970s with a new voice, one that belonged to young Californian screenwriter Tom Mankiewicz, whose flip, mordant, frequently macabre style would shape the next phase of 007's big screen career.

Producer Albert Broccoli wanted a strongly American sensibility for *Diamonds*. He was out to recapture the flavour of *Goldfinger*, a movie that now felt like a touchstone for Bond's crowd-pleasing glory days after the mixed reaction that met *On Her Majesty's Secret Service* (a film reclaimed as a classic in the decades since, but very much viewed as an anomaly at the time). *Goldfinger* helmer Guy Hamilton was duly enlisted and an early draft of the script pitched 007 against the bullion-hungering reprobate's twin brother. Blofeld's death-dealing satellite may well be a link to this original version of the tale, given Goldfinger's early adoption of laser technology in the 1964 film.

Diamonds brings us a brash bubblegum reality a world away from the European splendour of *OHMSS*. It's a film that feels distinctly tawdry in comparison with its predecessor. There's a queasy tone to its landscape of casinos and funeral homes, its cast of hustlers and hoods, and a sulphurous sense of bad taste that pervades everything from its freakshow Gorilla Girl to the shocking pink tie that Connery manfully attempts to rock. And as Bond bumps along desert scrubland in the weird, ungainly Moon buggy, pursued by chugging trikes, you can't help but feel that it's the most fundamentally inelegant Bond movie too.

VEGAS, BABY!

James Bond cuts an uncomfortable figure as he walks through the deep-pile, daylight-defying environment of a Las Vegas casino, accompanied by a soul-deadening serenade of piped muzak. If it's an attempt to chase a little Rat Pack cool, it feels belated, for Fleming's old world hero has arrived in Vegas just as the city has stopped swinging.

Once the playground of Sinatra and his equally sharp-suited cronies, Nevada's neon-soaked gaming capital now has a nasty polyester sheen. There's an existential emptiness in its world of gas stations, car lots and dollar motels that feels at odds with the traditional aspirational shimmer of the Bond universe. We may glimpse the unforgettable sight of an elephant playing a one-armed bandit but this all feels distinctly low-rent. Only as Connery rides a cable to the Whyte House, the Strip beyond alive with light against the desert night, does Vegas finally possess the sense of uncanny glamour that befits the screen's most stylish hero.

SHADES OF GRAY

Another Bond film, another Blofeld – and, familiar iconography of white cat and beige suit aside, another incarnation that feels utterly incompatible with its predecessors (though this Blofeld's obssession with plastic surgery and mischievous use of doubles at least hints at a possible rationale for all the identity-swapping).

Charles Gray played doomed Tokyo contact Dikko Henderson in *You Only Live Twice*. Two films later he returns as the new face of the SPECTRE mastermind, now blessed with a fine thatch of silver hair (were some of SPECTRE's extorted millions siphoned into hair replacement research?). Portly, louche and brandishing a cigarette holder, Gray brings an air of the gentleman's club to the role, relishing the foppish purr of such lines as "Right idea, Mr Bond... wrong pussy!" There's something incongruous about Gray disparaging Bond's Britain as "your pitiful little island" in a cut-glass English accent, but it fits with Fleming's original conception of Blofeld as an international shape-shifter.

A nameless cameo in *For Your Eyes Only* aside, it's the last we'll see of 007's arch enemy in the official movies until 2015's *Spectre*. With no final showdown between the two men in *Diamonds* the character will feel like unfinished business for decades.

THE ODD COUPLE

First seen observing a scorpion with the cold fascination of true psychopaths, Wint and Kidd, the homosexual hitmen, remain two of the most mesmerically off-beat characters in Bond history.

Played by Putter Smith, the flaxen-haired, walrus-moustached Mr Kidd is the first hint that Woodstock may have actually occurred in the heretofore impregnably establishment world of Bond. A jobbing musician, virgin actor Smith had actually played bass on numerous '60s pop classics, including Good Vibrations by the Beach Boys. Guy Hamilton spotted him working with Thelonious Monk at an LA jazz club. "I got a call about three months later and went down, thinking they wanted a bass sideline," Smith recalled. "They handed me a script and next thing you know I'm in a James Bond movie. I could not believe it!". In truth, Smith is miscast. There's no real menace in his performance – even advancing on Bond with a pair of flaming kebabs at the film's climax he radiates a gentle, sweet-natured hippy charm, as threatening as a bonged-out David Crosby.

Bruce Glover, however, is persuasively creepy as the touchy, cologne-spraying Mr Wint. Told to channel such classic screen villains as Sidney Greenstreet and Peter Lorre, he actually found his character through a sense of flashing-eyed possessiveness towards his partner: "Putter was my toy!"

INTERCEPTED INTELLIGENCE

The plot of *Diamonds Are Forever* was inspired by a dream of Cubby Broccoli's that his close friend Howard Hughes had been replaced by an imposter in his Vegas penthouse.

The reclusive Hughes proved an ally behind the scenes, pulling strings to close downtown Vegas for the film's showpiece car chase.

Singer-songwriter Paul Williams was the original choice for Mr Wint.

Raquel Welch was in the frame for the role of Tiffany Case.

Vegas mainstay Sammy Davis Jr cameoed in a scene that was later cut from the film, declaring of the tuxedo-clad Bond "They ain't never gonna get a cake big enough to put him on top of!"

Mr Wint originally jammed the scorpion into a man's mouth rather than place it down his shirt. It was judged to be too horrific.

Bond possesses a Playboy membership card.

Watch the scene where Bond is shown a Federal agent on guard in the hotel. "And Hamilton is right out here…" - that's actually director Guy Hamilton.

LIVE AND LET DIE

1973 121 minutes

Director: Guy Hamilton

Writer: Tom Mankiewicz

Score: George Martin

Title song: Paul McCartney and Wings

Cast: Roger Moore, Jane Seymour, Yaphet Kotto, Gloria Hendry, David Hedison

WE'VE BEEN EXPECTING YOU, MR MOORE

Roger Moore was always the heir apparent to James Bond. The wryly dashing Englishman had been on Broccoli and Saltzman's original shortlist for *Dr. No* and even played 007 in a sketch for Millicent Martin's 1964 comedy show *Mainly Millicent*. Winning small screen stardom as the Saint – popularly perceived as an extended screen test for Bond – Moore had been in the frame as recently as the late '60s, when the producers had approached him for an abortive version of *The Man With The Golden Gun*, set to be shot in Cambodia before civil war made filming in the region an impossibility. Tellingly, he had been Sean Connery's plus one for the premiere of *Diamonds Are Forever*, a choice that felt heavy with pop-cultural portent even then.

Connery's latest exodus was a potentially fatal wound to the heart of the franchise. Broccoli liked to disarm the egos of his leading men by reminding them that there had been an infinite parade of celluloid Tarzans, but George Lazenby's underwhelming box office proved that Bond was different. It needed to be a perfect fusion of part and performance, icon and star.

The studio, for its part, favoured an American. Paul Newman and Robert Redford were considered while Clint Eastwood opted to put himself out of the race: "To me, that was somebody else's gig," he later recalled. "That's Sean's deal. It didn't feel right for me to be doing it." In the end it came down to a simple choice between Roger Moore and rising star Burt Reynolds, whose breakout performance in 1972's *Deliverance* channelled a rugged, jungle-chested machismo that looked set to enshrine him as a genuine '70s action star. Director Guy Hamilton insisted that Reynolds possessed all the right qualities for Bond – "I must say the best people at the time were voting for Reynolds," screenwriter Tom Mankiewicz later revealed – but Broccoli vetoed him on the grounds that Bond must always be British (ironic, given he had originally signed American John Gavin for *Diamonds Are Forever*).

Roger Moore found himself haunted by Connery's voice on the immortal line "My name's Bond, James Bond" but aside from a flutter of nerves before his first press conference he embraced the chance to make Fleming's hero his own. "I didn't have any reservations – four or five thousand actors have played Hamlet!"

Intriguingly, Paul McCartney's title song instructs us to "give the other fella hell" – could this be the same "other fella" on George Lazenby's mind in *On Her Majesty's Secret Service*?

SHEER MAGNETISM

While Lazenby had been surrounded by the symbols and rituals of his predecessor – a move that only invited unflattering comparisons – Moore's blue-eyed incarnation of the superspy is introduced in a far craftier way.

Withheld from the pre-titles sequence, we finally find him in the creamily innocent arms of Madeline Smith, in his own bed, in Bond's singularly '70s bachelor pad (the camera lingers on him using a coffee maker in frankly pornographic detail). It's here that the movie smartly flips the traditional mission briefing scene, with M and Moneypenny encountering 007 on home turf, far from the familiar mahogany and leather of the spymaster's office – and, thankfully, far from the ghosts of the Connery films.

Edging on classic bedroom farce, complete with a girl in a wardrobe, it's a scene that plays to Moore's brilliance for light comedy, his eternal hint of a wink. "Sheer magnetism, darling," he purrs, saucily unzipping Madeline's dress with his latest Q-branch timepiece. Later he'll show us – and us alone – the rigged tarot deck that he uses to seduce Solitaire. Moore's almost conspiratorial with the audience, colluding in a smirky, knowing pact that softens the edges of the character. It's a very different approach to Connery, who frequently suggested a snarling disdain for his signature one-liners.

But Moore has a surprising toughness in his debut adventure. He threatens the life of Rosie Carver in a post-coital moment ("I certainly wouldn't have killed you before…") and by claiming Solitaire's virginity he steals away her psychic gift, an act of unmitigated bastardry beyond even Connery's Bond.

GHETTO FABULOUS

Live And Let Die is the first Bond film to chase and not define the big screen zeitgeist. It's a trend that would define the franchise over the next decade, from the nod to *Jaws* in *The Spy Who Loved Me* to the shameless Skywalking of *Moonraker*.

This is the age of *Shaft*, *Superfly* and *Foxy Brown* – trailblazers of the Blaxploitation fad that targeted a contemporary Afro-American audience with hip, ghetto-set adventures. Screenwriter Mankiewicz wanted to acknowledge the black revolution underway in America and threw out Fleming's original tale of a quest for pirate treasure – along with some unpalatable racial stereotypes – in favour of a contemporary, street level plot involving heroin smuggling.

Immaculate in Chesterfield coat, striped tie and leather gloves, Moore cuts a splendidly improbable figure in '70s Harlem, stepping from Savile Row across 110th St, the urbane colliding with the urban. The rusting, graffiti-scrawled back-alleys, loud pimp fashions and shopfronts filled with the leer of ritual skulls feel as exotic as anything we've ever glimpsed in a Bond film.

VOODOO CHARM

There's always been a distinct strain of sci-fi in Bond's big screen DNA, but *Live And Let Die* is the closest the franchise creeps towards horror. From the burning voodoo imagery of the opening titles to the whispering, scarecrow-haunted isle of San Monique, it's a film that carries a delicious occult shiver, quite at odds with Bond's traditionally rational universe.

The pre-titles sequence riffs on old Universal zombie movies, complete with goat-headed snake wrangler and Caribbean islanders losing themselves in the supernatural abandon of a ceremonial sacrifice. Elsewhere a hat with a totemically bloodied feather is left on a bed, utterly spooking a trained CIA operative (most hotels just leave chocolates on the pillow…).

At the heart of it all is the towering, taunting Baron Samedi, the single weirdest figure in Bond history. Introduced as "Voodoo god of cemeteries and chief of the legion of the dead – the man who cannot die", Samedi's booming laugh possesses a genuinely demonic sense of mischief. Is he flesh and blood or something more? The movie clearly suggests the latter. As he rises from a grave Bond pragmatically puts a bullet in his head. Samedi's eyes turn towards his own smouldering skull before Bond blasts the figure apart. Whatever it was, it wasn't human. Moments later another Samedi rises…

As played by Trinidadian dancer and choreographer Geoffrey Holder, the Baron is a memorable, unsettling presence, hi-jacking the final shot of the film as he rides a train into the end credits, laughing, eternally laughing, at the certainties of Bond's world.

WELCOME TO PEPPERLAND

While *Diamonds Are Forever* brought a broader, darker sense of humour to the Bonds, the arrival of blustering redneck sheriff J W Pepper may be the precise moment the franchise remodels itself as comedy spectacle.

In truth the tub-bellied Louisiana lawman is a great comic turn by Clifton James, a New Yorker and a graduate of Lee Strasberg's prestigious Actor's Studio. Spitting huge wads of tobacco-stained phlegm, tongue protruding like a sun-bothered bulldog, sweat-drenched face forever dabbed by a hanky, Pepper is every redneck inch the anti-Bond – and a perfect foil for Roger Moore.

Inspiring Jackie Gleason's Sheriff Buford T Justice in 1977's *Smokey And The Bandit* – starring nearly-Bond Burt Reynolds – he points the way to a whole sub-genre of raucous, stunt-crammed, Southern-fried fare that would find great success on screens both big and small in the late '70s, from *Every Which Way But Loose* to *The Dukes Of Hazzard*.

TRESPASSERS WILL BE EATEN

It's the most gloriously pulpy moment in the Bonds to date. Marooned on a rock at Kananga's heroin farm, 007 watches as the snouts of crocodiles surface from the rust-coloured water, their dark eyes fixing upon him with unmistakably hungry

72

intent. For once his Q-issued gadgetry is useless. Stealthily, a croc clambers onto the rock, followed by another, then another... How will he get out of this one, kids?

Producer Harry Saltzman suggested a helicopter rescue. Screenwriter Mankiewicz dismissed it as "too easy" – though he had absolutely no idea how to resolve the cliffhanger he'd written himself into. "Why the hell doesn't he jump over their backs?" suggested Ross Kananga, owner of the true life crocodile farm that provided the location and the man who loaned his name to the movie's villain.

On New Year's Eve 1972 Kananga actually attempted the insanely dangerous stunt himself, taking five heart-stopping attempts to leap across the backs of the snapping, increasingly agitated predators. The audacious final sequence is a triumph, an adrenalin hit of pure cinematic thrills.

INTERCEPTED INTELLIGENCE

Tom Mankiewicz's original choice for Solitaire was Diana Ross.

The screenplay tells us that Tee Hee's arm was taken by a crocodile named Old Albert – a sly nod to producer Albert R Broccoli.

Moore chose to wear crocodile shoes in the scene where he's surrounded by the crocs. He soon regretted this.

Clifton James wore stomach padding for his role as gutbucket sheriff J W Pepper.

The script takes pains to avoid direct comparisons with the Connery years. Bond orders a "Bourbon, no ice," rather than his familiar vodka martini.

The crew fretted that there was a real voodoo curse on the production – Roger Moore was incapacitated by kidney stones while a showpiece boat chase in the bayou saw stunts go wrong.

Moore wrote an account of his time filming the movie. Roger Moore As James Bond 007 was published by Pan Books in 1973 to tie in with the film's release.

The filmmakers considered bringing original Bond girl Ursula Andress back as Honey Ryder to help ease the transition to the new 007.

THE MAN WITH THE GOLDEN GUN

1974 125 minutes

Director: Guy Hamilton

Writers: Richard Maibaum, Tom Mankiewicz

Score: John Barry

Title song: Lulu

Cast: Roger Moore, Maud Adams, Christopher Lee, Britt Ekland, Hervé Villechaize

"A DUEL BETWEEN TITANS"

Live And Let Die was a hit, and the Bondmakers scrambled to capitalise on their new 007.

Roger Moore's encore mission was a fast-tracked adaptation of Ian Fleming's final Bond novel, published posthumously in 1965. "I had always envisioned it as a classic shoot-out; as *Shane*, if you will," said screenwriter Tom Mankiewicz, who walked from the project after the first draft, citing personal conflict with director Guy Hamilton.

For all the sun-struck dazzle of its Thai locations it's a film that feels distinctly undercooked. There's a gutsy bluster to the title song but the credits sequence that accompanies it feels tired and uninspired, like a showgirl whose heart just isn't in it anymore.

Elsewhere the movie brazenly reheats elements that made *Live And Let Die* popular: Bond steals a speedboat in a bid to replay the bayou boat chase while redneck sheriff J W Pepper returns, implausibly relocated from Louisiana to Thailand as the ugly-shirted Tourist from Hell. Britt Ekland is even locked in a wardrobe, just like Madeline Smith.

And, once again, a Bond film feels reactive, its martial arts trimmings in debt to the Bruce Lee-inspired boom that also brought us Hammer's *Legend Of The Seven Golden Vampires*, Marvel's *Master Of Kung Fu* comic book and Carl Douglas's number one single Kung Fu Fighting. It's all deeply 1974. Ironically, the film's plot revolves around the contemporary energy crisis. Despite the star wattage of Roger Moore, the Bond franchise looks to be having an energy crisis of its own.

HE HAS A POWERFUL WEAPON...

Veteran Hollywood gunslinger Jack Palance was an early candidate for the role of triple-nippled master assassin Francisco Scaramanga. Christopher Lee eventually won the glittering pistol, bringing the familiar chill of his Dracula gaze to the Bond universe.

"We have so much in common, Mr Bond," he claims – and it's true. Trim and cultivated, a world away from the thug of Fleming's novel, this Scaramanga is the shadow-Bond, a man with a self-appointed licence to kill.

Is government bureaucracy all that separates him from 007? It's a thought that provokes a steely flash of morality from Bond himself: "When I kill it's on specific orders of my government, and those I kill are themselves killers." You can certainly imagine the pair sharing a dry martini in some smoke-and-leather Piccadilly club but when Scaramanga's claim to be a gentleman is met by Bond's comment "I doubt if you qualify on that score" it's a rebuke that visibly wounds the pistol king.

DANSE MACABRE

The Man With The Golden Gun is a film saturated with the macabre.

Soundtracked by honky-tonk piano, Scaramanga's murderous, kaleidoscopic funhouse feels like something from *The Avengers* at its most surreal and darkly carnivalesque. All that hypnotic iconography of giant eyeballs, swirling circles and doors to nowhere could equally be torn straight from *The Twilight Zone*. Bond's world has never seemed so treacherously strange – MI6 sets up base within the off-kilter remains of RMS Queen Elizabeth, wax effigies of sumo wrestlers come to life in a garden at night and a woman sits in the centre of a cheering crowd, a single bullethole in her chest, frozen in the moment of her own murder.

The film's eeriest scene finds Bond staring at shopfront televisions in an empty, neon-lit street, only to see bowler-hatted homunculus Nick Nack smile at him from a screen. As John Barry's uneasy score reminds us, this secret shadow-world of Bond's is one of eternal, unshakable danger, only ever one golden bullet away from death.

CUT TO THE VILLECHAIZE

First glimpsed almost toppling beneath a tray of Moët, Scaramanga's lethal factotum is one of the most unforgettable Bond icons. Much of this is, naturally, down to the unconventional physicality of Hervé Villechaize, the 3' 11" French-born actor who brought the ever-immaculate henchman to life.

Villechaize was an aspiring artist, photographer and occasional Off Broadway performer who was working as a rat catcher's assistant in South Central Los Angeles when his life-changing Bond break came. By all accounts he partied hard on location in Thailand, propelled by a libido that would leave Bond himself feeling undersexed.

As a character, Nick Nack has a conflicted, taunting relationship with his gun-toting master. Mocking and malicious, his loyalties ever shifting, he prowls the movie like some tormenting storybook imp.

BACK FOR MOORE

Roger Moore continues to define the '70s Bond in *The Man With The Golden Gun*. There's a winning boyishness that's so very different to Connery – he adjusts his tie when a bellydancer tells him he's handsome, a signature tic of his light comedy style and another of Moore's little winks to the audience that he's not taking it all terribly seriously.

It's not all dancing eyebrow and irony, though. This Bond bleeds in the fight with the goons in the dressing room and elsewhere there's a conscious attempt to darken his characterisation. He threatens Andrea Anders with a surprising physicality and slaps her hard in the face when she frustrates him. Moore and the screenwriters would come to regret this, considering such bounder behaviour a bad fit for their charming leading man. Certainly Moore's Bond would never be quite so brutal on screen again.

"EVER HEARD OF EVEL KNIEVEL?"

Golden Gun's setpiece stunt finds Bond corkscrewing a car across a broken bridge, a spluttering, bacon-faced J W Pepper in tow. Yes, it's slightly spoilt by a daft swanee whistle sound effect – John Barry's only misstep – but it remains one of the great showstoppers in the franchise's history.

Stunt co-ordinator WJ Milligan Jr originally created the Astro Spiral jump for a show at the Houston Aerodrome. He started designing the 360 degree turn in 1971, feeding records of highway accidents into an IBM computer to calculate a formula for a ramp that would provide the optimum angle for the leap. The car needed to be perfectly balanced, with the steering wheel placed in the exact centre of the vehicle.

"Bumps" Willett performed the stunt, lying beneath a pair of dummies, controlling the car with his feet. He did it in one take, watched by an anxious Roger Moore. Hamilton thought it was too perfect and asked him to do it again. Willett refused. It was the first time he'd ever attempted it.

INTERCEPTED INTELLIGENCE

While Fleming's novel was set in Jamaica, the producers toyed with the idea of shooting in Iran before settling on Thailand.

Christopher Lee was Ian Fleming's cousin, and an early choice for the role of Dr No.

The movie's Phuket location work opened up the islands to the global tourism industry.

There's a brief reprise of the *Live And Let Die* soundtrack when Pepper first spots Bond.

Scaramanga's golden gun is pieced together from a fountain pen, a cigarette lighter, a cigarette case and a cuff-link. Lee struggled with the assembly, calling it "a wretched gun."

This was the first Bond film to be screened at the Kremlin.

THE SPY WHO LOVED ME

1977 125 minutes

Director: Lewis Gilbert

Writers: Christopher Wood, Richard Maibaum

Score: Marvin Hamlisch

Title song: Carly Simon

Cast: Roger Moore, Barbara Bach, Curt Jurgens, Richard Kiel, Caroline Munro

NOBODY DOES IT BETTER

The tenth Bond movie shares a title with Ian Fleming's tenth Bond novel – but there the resemblance ends.

The original tale is an uncharacteristic 007 adventure, a first person narrative told from the perspective of Vivienne Michel, a woman menaced by mobsters in a remote American motel. Bond only appears in the final third, almost a chivalric dream figure ("He had come from nowhere, like the prince in the fairy tales, and he had saved me from the dragon"). Bruised by the book's reception, Fleming forbade the filmmakers from using any part of it except the title (an abridged version

appeared in low-rent men's mag Stag, retitled Motel Nymph –
just imagine that on a Leicester Square billboard).

Despite a throwaway reference to nuclear submarines in
Fleming's original story, the filmmakers mulled a bewildering
array of potential plotlines. One early pitch saw the overthrow
of SPECTRE's old guard by a new, more politically motivated
generation of terrorists. A sly Anthony Burgess proposed Bond
foil an extortion plot that would force the Queen to strip on live
TV. Other dead end plot elements included Loch Ness, the
return of *From Russia With Love*'s Tatiana Romanova and a
villainous lair in the Norwegian fjords.

Cubby Broccoli certainly felt significant creative
pressure to make this one work. It was to be his first solo
production credit after the dissolution of his partnership with
longtime comrade-in-Bondage Harry Saltzman. And Broccoli
delivered: *The Spy Who Loved Me* reclaims the sense of
widescreen grandeur that once defined the franchise. It's a
movie possessed of staggering self-belief, a towering
confidence in the power of 007. "Baby, you're the best,"
reassures Carly Simon's title song, an exercise in pure male
fantasy ego-stroking where even the piano keys seem to swoon
admiringly. It was a declaration of empowerment echoed by
the boast on the poster: "It's the biggest, it's the best, it's
Bond... and beyond!"

And, for once, it was.

TWICE TOLD TALE

"Twice is the only way to live!" panted the tagline to *You Only Live Twice*, a philosophy brazenly embraced by the Bondmakers a decade later. *The Spy Who Loved Me* is essentially a Xerox of 1967's Connery era epic: Blofeld steals space capsules while Stromberg snaffles nuclear subs, but both scoundrels plot to engineer a war between the world's superpowers. The two movies also share design touches (monorails and boilersuited goons), identical story beats and even the same director in Lewis Gilbert, who would recycle it all again in 1979's *Moonraker*.

Other echoes of classic Bond include a sub-aquatic skirmish (*Thunderball*), a ski chase (*On Her Majesty's Secret Service*), a gadget-laden spymobile (*Goldfinger*) and a fight on a train (*From Russia With Love*). *The Spy Who Loved Me* is 007's Greatest Hits album, remixing and remastering past glories. But there are new flavours here, too: the competitive edge between our hero and Soviet agent Anya redefines the usual dynamic, close to screwball comedy in places.

Gilbert has an impish touch as director – cutting the Bond theme at the exact moment 007 cuts the monitors in Stromberg's operations room – but also impresses when it comes to the action. Packed with pyrotechnics, stuntwork and gunfire, the sequence where Bond and the navy take the supertanker has the power and energy of a Great British war movie.

INTO THE JAWS OF DEATH

Bond films now ride the pop culture slipstream - we've already seen *Live And Let Die*'s Blaxploitation chic and *Golden Gun*'s co-opting of the martial arts craze - so it's no surprise that *Spy*'s henchman nods to Spielberg's beach-clearing 1975 blockbuster, *Jaws*.

While the seed of the character can be found in the original novel – Fleming sketches a brutish, steel-mouthed hood named Horror – it's all 7' 2" of Richard Kiel that enshrines Jaws in the pantheon of Bond rogues. We shiver as he feasts vampirically in the Egyptian night or clasps his hand like a huge ham around Roger Moore's face – then smile as he strides away from certain death once more, a hulking Wile E Coyote, dusting down his blazer and adjusting his tie like some Bizarro version of Bond. Those tiny character notes are everything. It's the outsized Kiel's lightness of touch that makes this henchman immortal.

THINKING BIG

The Spy Who Loved Me finds the Bond movies dreaming on an unprecedented scale. There's a brilliant, monstrous grandeur to production designer Ken Adam's sets (he was forced to build a vast new soundstage in order to house his vision for Stromberg's supertanker lair). It's a world one step removed from reality, where a Soviet spymaster's HQ is a Russian fairytale castle and a web-fingered shipping magnate's base rises from the waves like some towering technological spider.

Director Lewis Gilbert masterfully corrals the spectacle, placing Bond in equally breathtaking true life locations, from the clear waters of the Bahamas to a ruined Egyptian temple. Alongside *Moonraker*, *Spy*'s unofficial sequel, this is the last gasp of Bond as marquee spectacle before the franchise downsizes in the 1980s.

"THE THINGS I DO FOR ENGLAND"

Spy immediately wins over its audience with a stone cold showstopper, the most audacious opener of any Bond film – and, at a cost of $500,000, the single priciest stunt at that point in cinema history.

Stuntman Rick Sylvester pocketed $30,000 for his daredevil ski-jump, staged on the vertiginous peak of Mount Asgard on Baffin Island in the Northern Canadian territories (3000 feet and one take, no less). While Guy Hamilton dubbed a swanee whistle over *Golden Gun*'s setpiece car stunt, Gilbert wisely frames this heart-stopping moment in absolute silence. But it's 007's slow-blooming Union Jack parachute that provides the killer punchline, a crowd-pleasing piece of flag-waving perfectly timed for the Silver Jubilee year of 1977. It's an image that carries a certain degree of irony, of course, given the country's economic decay, but in that one glorious, hilarious gag, our national hero keeps the British end up with style to spare.

ROGER ROGER

Roger Moore's third shot at Bond is his best, a seamless fusion of star and part.   Gilbert thought that Moore was being made to echo Connery in his previous movies so set out to cultivate something a little smoother, funnier and distinctly more English. Moore doles out the double entendres like smut-dusted bonbons, mining unimagined stratas of filth in such seemingly innocuous phrases as "Well, let me enlarge your vocabulary..." Watch his eyes swivel and twinkle like innuendo-hunting radar as Barbara Bach asks "Why don't you lie down and let me look at it?"

Moore owns *The Spy Who Loved Me*, always charmingly aware of his own implausibility but able to summon moments of ice and humanity, too (he tells Anya that he killed her lover as an act of cold professionalism, but flinches at her mention of his dead wife). He can't quite pull off that canary yellow ski-suit, mind.

"ONE OR TWO RATHER SPECIAL ACCESSORIES…"

Bond's Lotus Esprit races like a pearl bullet around the coast roads of Sardinia, hunted by a helicopter gun-ship flirtatiously commanded by Hammer fox Caroline Munro. After a breathless, white-knuckling chase sequence Bond guns it in a seemingly suicidal plunge from a pier. With our hearts in our mouths, we watch as it flips into submersible mode, sprouting propellers and fins and dispensing harpoons and depth charges like some deadly collision between Captain Nemo and *Top Gear*.

It's a '70s dream of a car, Concorde-sleek and audaciously modern. While Sean Connery's Bond was forever linked to the old world quicksilver elegance of an Aston Martin DB5 there's something profoundly Space: 1977 about Moore's choice of wheels. It seems to belong to a Britain where Gerry Anderson is Prime Minister and there's a statue of Dan Dare on a spare plinth in Trafalgar Square. You might imagine it being assembled by robots to the sound of Jean Michel Jarre.

Of course there are those snide souls who claim Lotus stands for Lots Of Trouble, Usually Serious. But then isn't that the most perfect motto for James Bond?

INTERCEPTED INTELLIGENCE

Anya's Russian lover in the pre-titles is played by Michael Billington, who was once in the frame for the role of Bond himself.

John Landis was one of the screenwriters who pitched ideas for the film.

Spy is credited to Christopher Wood, who created the saucy *Confessions* series under the name Timothy Lea. Wood's original screenplay portrays Bond as a harder-edged character who threatens Fekesh's girlfriend with a gun rather than deploying Moore charm.

Japan was a potential location (Gilbert considered using the Okinawa sea lab as Stromberg's base).

The production faced an injunction suit from *Thunderball* producer Kevin McClory, who felt it strayed too close to *Warhead*, his own attempt to remake that movie. The

Bondmakers retained their claim to an underwater setting but all references to Blofeld and SPECTRE were excised.

Five cameras covered the ski jump. Only one caught the stunt.

Lewis Gilbert developed a crick in his neck from looking up at the towering Richard Kiel.

Stanley Kubrick advised Ken Adam on how best to light the mammoth supertanker set on the newly built 007 Stage.

Sandor is played by former wrestler Milton Reid, who was also one of the henchmen in *Dr. No*.

MOONRAKER

1979 126 minutes

Director: Lewis Gilbert

Writer: Christopher Wood

Score: John Barry

Title song: Shirley Bassey

Cast: Roger Moore, Lois Chiles, Michael Lonsdale, Richard Kiel, Corinne Cléry

"WHERE ALL THE OTHER BONDS END... THIS ONE BEGINS!"

Hurling 007 to the stars, *Moonraker* is the most outlandish of all the Bonds. Ian Fleming's original novel seems positively prosaic in comparison: first published in 1953, the third Bond adventure is rooted in the gloom of postwar Britain, a land threatened by the ghost of Nazi rocket science where Bond operates as a kind of lustier, more conflicted Biggles. Our hero never ventures beyond England's grey-green shores, fails to bed the heroine and finds himself embroiled in a four-chapter bridge game – all far from the raw material of blockbuster cinema.

Cubby Broccoli spurned Fleming's plot with an uncharacteristic flash of disdain for the source material – "A little piddling rocket that went up to destroy London" – but channeled the villainous Hugo Drax's Nazi past into a tale of a madman chasing a master race fantasy high in Earth orbit.

Drax's dream of establishing a race of gods by annihilating life on Earth is the grandest, most diabolically high-stakes plot Bond has ever confronted, and the filmmakers had ambition to match. The total cost of the eleventh Bond adventure was greater than the combined budgets of the entire run of '60s films. Very much an amped-up sequel to the crowd-pleasing spectacle of *The Spy Who Loved Me*, *Moonraker* is Bond as pure widescreen fantasia.

WHERE NO BOND HAS GONE BEFORE

In 1977 the closing moments of *The Spy Who Loved Me* promised "James Bond will return in *For Your Eyes Only*". And then a phenomenon named *Star Wars* smashed into pop culture, shaking up the traditional certainties of Bond's universe.

Colonising the minds of Force-struck kids everywhere, the success of George Lucas's movie established a blockbuster arms race in late '70s cinema. As studios scrambled to profit from the SF craze – *Close Encounters Of The Third Kind* and

Superman The Movie arrived in its slipstream, with *Star Trek: The Motion Picture* and *Alien* readying for launch – Broccoli jettisoned *Eyes* in favour of another unfilmed Fleming title, the suitably spacey-sounding Moonraker.

The film winks at the space fantasy boom as much as it blatantly steals from it. An entry-coder in a secret lab is keyed with John Williams's five-note *Close Encounters* theme while a silhouetted girl in the title sequence soars like a Kryptonian superhero in red and blue. Elsewhere Bond saves the day by "switching to manual" (you can almost hear a disembodied Alec Guinness whisper "Use the Force, James!").

For diehards the decision to propel Fleming's hero into orbit was a bandwagon-jump too far. And yes, there's something jarring about hearing the zap of laser weapons in a Bond film . But it's as utterly of its time as the disco mix of Shirley Bassey's keening title song that accompanies the end credits. As the poster had it, "Outer space now belongs to 007" – a clear declaration of territorial intent to the Lucas empire.

THE MOORE BOND'S THE MERRIER?

"People go to laugh at Bond films," insisted director Lewis Gilbert, unapologetically. And the popular perception of *Moonraker* is that it's the apogee of all that's deemed ridiculous about the Roger Moore era: Fleming's tortured government assassin remade as a safari-suited cheese, strolling merrily between slapstick set-pieces, an unstoppable gatling-gun of smirks and double-entendres. But is that fair?

There's actually considerably more to *Moonraker* than double-taking comedy pigeons and candy-striped hover-gondolas (yes, officially the moment it all goes too far). Take the scene where Bond staggers from a near-fatal spin in the rigged centrifuge machine. He emerges slick with sweat, visibly shaken, stripped of his quips, his eternally arched (and arch) eyebrow finally quelled. He falls, but is too proud to let Holly help him. Bond exits in silence, half-broken, momentarily closer to the Fleming original than Connery ever came.

Elsewhere Corinne's pursuit by Drax's hounds is the grimmest, most nightmarish sequence in all the Bonds. As daylight cuts through a tangle of trees a pack of dogs race a terrified girl to her death, accompanied by a John Barry score that sounds like some beautiful, regretful lament. As the dogs fall on Corinne we cut to the bells of Venice. It's as if the film itself wants to outrun the dark realities of Bond's world. Once again, no one's laughing.

SKY FALL

The ski-jump that launched *The Spy Who Loved Me* set a new standard in grandstanding opening setpieces. *Moonraker* competes with an equally audacious pre-titles gag: Bond is pushed out of an aeroplane and, armed only with blazer, slacks and his wits, engages in a fearless freefall tussle for a parachute, high above the fast-approaching ground.

It misses the brilliant, iconic kick of *Spy*'s Union Jack punchline – though Moore, amusingly, appears to be manoeuvering through the air by the cunningly applied use of flares at one point – but it's an impressive piece of stunt-craft that took no less than 88 separate skydives to accomplish.

The filmmakers faced some crucial practical challenges: could parachutes be made small enough to fit beneath the stunt performers' clothes? And would a Panavision camera prove too heavy for aerial photography? Skydiving specialist BJ Worth developed a parachute pack that was only 25mm thick and, quite by chance, the crew found an old, experimental Panavision camera (fitted with a plastic lens, not a glass one) in a Paris pawn shop.

Stuntman Jake Lombard assumes the role of 007 in the scene and while his doubling may be a little too conspicuous at times it's an acceptable trade for one of the most genuinely courageous stunts in the Bond canon.

JAWS 2

Moonraker marks the return of Richard Kiel as the hulking, steel-mouthed killer from *The Spy Who Loved Me*. It's the first (and only time) that a henchman is allowed an encore performance in the Bond movies. While the original screenplay for *Spy* had conclusively killed the character, Broccoli, sensing his potential, chose to spare him from his fatally ironic encounter with a Great White in Stromberg's shark pool.

"I had convinced the producer that Jaws should have some characteristics that were human to counteract the steel teeth," recalled Kiel. "I guess I overdid it – I became too likeable to kill off!" In truth Jaws is not best served by *Moonraker*, too often reduced to a gurning comedy stooge whose ultimate redemption as an ally of Bond's strikes an improbably cosy note for a character originally established as a professional murderer (whatever next, tea and fig rolls with Rosa Klebb?).

But go back to the wonderfully macabre scene where he infiltrates the Rio street carnival beneath a giant, bobbing clown head. Advancing on the lone Manuela down an empty, darkened alleyway he's legitimately terrifying, a figure plucked from the realm of nightmare, not *Looney Tunes*.

THE FINAL FRONTIER

Key to the sci-fi-spiced iconography of *Moonraker* is the space shuttle. In the real world it wouldn't launch until 1981, but NASA's creation was already embedded in the public consciousness as the future of space travel. Its inclusion gave this Bond adventure a cool, topical gleam.

While the end credits slyly declared "And on location – in outer space!" it was veteran British modelmaker Derek Meddings who sent 007 starwards. Broccoli had originally approached the big American FX houses and while he was wowed by their technical acumen he baulked at their call for a stake in the film's profits. Meddings approached the task with characteristic ingenuity: magnesium flares simulated launch-fire while cascades of salt doubled for the contrails of the shuttle in flight. The climactic destruction of Drax's space station was accomplished with the timely creative input of twelve-bore shotguns.

Meddings's methods may have been far from the bleeding edge of Industrial Light and Magic but the results remain startling, from the shuttle's stately escape from Earth's blue grip to the heart-stopping moment Drax's orbital lair emerges from darkness, ominous and insectile in the firmament. Teamed with Barry's most majestic score it truly feels like a thrilling new frontier for Bond.

INTERCEPTED INTELLIGENCE:

The production originally hoped to film aboard a genuine NASA shuttle launch.

Derek Meddings's FX work earned an Academy Award nomination – it lost to *Alien*.

Lois (Moneypenny) Maxwell's daughter Melinda is one of Drax's master race.

Jaws was originally to fall in love with a 7' 7" Amazonian.

The fight between Bond and Chang in the glass factory was a revised version of a scene cut from *The Spy Who Loved Me*, where Bond brawled in a museum of Egyptian antiquities.

The space art director on *Moonraker* was Harry Lange, who had headed NASA's future projects division in the 1960s, working alongside rocket pioneer Werner Von Braun. He had been production designer on *2001: A Space Odyssey*.

Early contenders for the title song were Kate Bush, Johnny Mathis and Frank Sinatra – "Fly Me To The Moonraker"?

FOR YOUR EYES ONLY

1981 127 minutes

Director: John Glen

Writers: Michael G Wilson, Richard Maibaum

Score: Bill Conti

Title song: Sheena Easton

Cast: Roger Moore, Carole Bouquet, Julian Glover, Topol, Lynn Holly Johnson

KEEPING IT REAL

For Your Eyes Only is an emphatic reality check for the Bond franchise. A grounded, almost mundane counterpoint to the escalating excess of the '70s, it's a film that rewrites our hero's family motto - for now, the world is clearly enough.

Gone are the grand lairs of the villains, the whimsically macabre henchmen, the fantastical gadgetry and planet-threatening schemes, replaced by a modest tale of drug smuggling, personal vendettas and low-key Cold War maneuvering. Tellingly, Bond's Lotus is destroyed in an early scene, forcing him to endure a slapstick-packed chase sequence in a Citroen 2CV, a set of wheels more suited to the school run than the adrenalised world of international espionage.

It's an unexpected swerve for the movies. *Moonraker* had been a global hit, perfectly attuned to the post-*Star Wars* landscape. With fantasy cinema in the ascendant, the decision to strip Bond of the improbable was a genuine box office gamble, but executive producer Michael G Wilson (Broccoli's stepson, and a rising creative force within Eon) was troubled by 007's growing disconnect from reality. Inspired by the classic spycraft of *From Russia With Love*, he was determined to return Fleming's creation to core values, to humanise this suave, unbreakable superman and clip his Q-branch wings.

THE FLEMING FACTOR

While *The Spy Who Loved Me* and *Moonraker* had conspicuously outdreamt their source material, Moore's fifth film marks a reverent retreat to the work of Bond's creator.

The title homages Fleming's first anthology of short stories – adaptations of episodes he'd outlined for an abortive 007 TV series in the '50s - and the screenplay splices two of those five yarns: "Risico", an account of an Italian dope-smuggling racket that gives us the characters of Kristatos and Columbo, and the title tale itself, the story of Judy Havelock (more exotically named Melina in the movie, and armed with a

100

funky crossbow in place of Fleming's choice of bow and arrow), out to avenge her parents' murder at the hands of Cuban hitmen.

The movie also plunders another piece of unfilmed Fleming. The sequence where Bond and Melina suffer the ordeal of keel-hauling is recycled from the novel of Live And Let Die. Coincidentally, 1981 saw the resurrection of the literary Bond with the publication of John Gardner's Licence Renewed, the first officially sanctioned post-Fleming adventure since 1968's Colonel Sun. The drably credible, Saab-driving agent in its pages feels in synch with the newly grounded incarnation on the big screen. This was the redefined face of Bond for the recession-bruised Britain of the early '80s. A more modest hero, to be sure.

FLOWERS FOR TRACY

For Your Eyes Only aims to erase the lingering smirk of *Moonraker*.

Its mission to humanise Bond is established from the opening frames of the pre-titles sequence, which place him by the grave of his late wife, Tracy. It's hard to say what's more jolting: Roger Moore in uncharacteristically sombre, reflective mood, the Betjemanesque location of the English churchyard (a reminder of how rarely we see Bond on home shores, and never in such an *Avengers*-style heritage setting) or the explicit continuity with 1969's *On Her Majesty's Secret Service*.

An impressive helicopter sequence follows, thrusting Bond into the ugly heartland of industrial London. This feels like jarringly new territory too. Spiritually, the pipes and chimney stacks of the abandoned Beckton gasworks surely belong to the urban milieu of *The Sweeney* or *The Professionals* (this is certainly the only Bond movie to flaunt a deeply unexotic credit for "North Thames Gas Board" – not quite Fleming, is it?).

The villain of this sequence is ultimately revealed as a bald, cat-stroking maniac in a wheelchair – a cheeky nod to Blofeld, the former cornerstone of the franchise now ensnared in the ongoing legal battle with rival filmmaker Kevin McClory. The world's still waiting for an explanation of his baffling line "I'll buy you a delicatessen – in stainless steel!"

ENTER JOHN GLEN

Eyes is the first 007 adventure by John Glen, the director who would come to define James Bond for the '80s with a decade-long, five-film sequence that still stands as the longest unbroken run of any helmer.

As with most Broccoli-anointed talent he was promoted from within. Glen had served as action unit director on a number of previous Bonds, supervising the bobsleigh sequence in *OHMSS* and capturing the heart-stopping ski-jump in *The Spy Who Loved Me*. He was a fan of the Fleming novels and in synch with the producers' desire to root the series in a muscular sense of reality.

There's rust in the Bond universe now, from the gasworks smoke stacks of the pre-titles sequence to the ocean-stained hulk of naval vessel St Georges. This new sense of reality extends to the shocking smears of blood we glimpse on the corpses of the Havelocks, brutally slain on the deck of their boat. Glen has a journeyman rep but there are some striking visuals here - a claw-handed diving suit looks alien and monstrous in one of the film's tensest scenes - and he also proves to have a fine eye for locations, from the shimmering Ionian sea to the rugged peaks of Greece. If *Eyes* lacks the velvet grandeur of classic Bond it does at least succeed as photogenic travel porn.

Elsewhere, Glen's touch is less sure. An inescapable hint of '80s wine bar haunts the film's attempts at romantic sophistication while a comedy coda with a marigolds-clad Margaret Thatcher and sprout-stealing Denis shamelessly plays to the cheap seats, distinctly at odds with the film's quest to purge the kitschier elements of big screen Bond.

MOUNTAIN MAN

Bond's plummet from the edge of Kristatos's mountaintop lair proves the film's most memorable piece of stuntwork. For once the absence of music underscores the drama – all we hear is the ceaseless howl of the wind and the desperate chink of gunbarrel on grappling hooks as Bond fights to rescale the precipice.

The fall from the rockface was enacted for real, with in-house daredevil Rick Sylvester (who had performed *Spy*'s ski-jump) doubling for a vertigo-cursed Roger Moore, who was mainlining valium and warm beer simply to perform on the mountain, let alone plunge from it. While Sylvester had agreed to the potentially fatal stunt he soon realised he had no real idea how to accomplish it. In a panic he sought out veteran FX man Derek Meddings, who knocked up a special rig and a landing trough with sandbags.

When the day came to shoot the dizzying fall, a superstitious Sylvester did his best to avoid the unbeatable aerial view of the local cemetery.

THE NEW BOND?

For Your Eyes Only very nearly saw a fourth actor strap on the iconic shoulder holster. Certainly the tabloids were confident that surly *Professionals* star Lewis Collins was in the frame for the most coveted gig on the British screen (Collins was indeed a contender but later confessed he'd had a less than auspicious meeting with Broccoli, who found him "too aggressive": "I was in his office for five minutes, but it was really over for me in seconds. I have heard since that he doesn't like me. That's unfair. He's expecting another Connery to walk through the door and there are few of them around.").

The opening callback to Tracy's grave was designed to cement a sense of continuity for any new 007, but in the event Roger Moore signed at the last hour – much to the relief of John Glen, who had dreaded the prospect of breaking in a neophyte Bond on his first watch as director.

Moore's reluctance to return to Bondage may have been as much to do with an honest awareness of his gathering age as his traditional blink-and-you-lose money game with Broccoli. He was particularly perturbed by the idea of co-star Lynn Holly Johnson playing a nymphomaniac teen – "I thought I was a bit long-in-the-tooth even then," he later admitted – and the film takes care to reposition Bond in her presence. The usually remorseless seducer resists Bibi's advances with the deathless line "Yes, well, you get your clothes on and I'll buy you an ice cream…"

Moore clashed with Glen over the moment Bond boots Locque's car over a cliff, consigning the henchman to his death. The star felt it was too vicious, too callous – not "Roger

Moore Bond". Glen disagreed, keen to steel-cap the edges of Moore's louche persona. He won.

INTERCEPTED INTELLIGENCE

Tracy's gravestone is engraved with the words "We have all the time in the world" – a direct quote from *On Her Majesty's Secret Service*, as well as the title of its love song.

Main villain Julian Glover was once considered for the role of Bond himself.

The anonymous Blofeld surrogate is played by John Hollis – Lobot in *The Empire Strikes Back*.

Bond's not entirely without gadgets in this one – he has a transmitter watch.

John Glen's inspiration for the opening helicopter sequence came from a Pinewood technician he'd seen playing with a remote control car.

The monks of the Meteora monastery attempted to sabotage the location shoot. The filmmakers built their own monastery on a neighbouring rock.

Blondie had a stab at the title song but rising star Sheena Easton, then known for BBC documentary series *The Big Time*, ultimately won the gig.

OCTOPUSSY

1983 131 minutes

Director: John Glen

Writers: George MacDonald Fraser, Michael G Wilson, Richard Maibaum

Score: John Barry

Title song: Rita Coolidge

Cast: Roger Moore, Maud Adams, Louis Jourdan, Steven Berkoff, Kristina Wayborn

KEEPING UP WITH THE JONESES

If *Moonraker* had chased the rocket trail of *Star Wars* then *Octopussy* was a landgrab for another corner of the Lucas empire.

1981's *Raiders Of The Lost Ark* had redefined the modern action film. It resurrected the knuckle-bruising, globe-hopping spirit of Saturday matinee adventure and fused it with a slick, movie brat generation understanding of cinema to build the ultimate celluloid thrill machine. In an irony that Cubby Broccoli must have found especially vexing, Spielberg made *Raiders* to exorcise his frustration at being refused the chance to direct a 007 adventure. "I told him I wanted to do a Bond picture more than anything else in the world," Spielberg recalled, "and he said, 'We only hire British, experienced directors.'"

Octopussy steals some of Indy's pulp adventure mojo: India's vibrant marketplaces and spider-haunted jungles bring a *Gunga Din* sense of colonial period adventure and there's a distinct hint of Belloq in the silky, urbane menace of Kamal Khan. We have a character who declares "I hate snakes!" and a a taxi vanishes behind a hastily erected awning, just like the truck in *Raiders*. But *Octopussy* foreshadows as much as it pickpockets: 1984's *Indiana Jones And The Temple Of Doom* finds the two-fisted archaeologist following Bond to the subcontinent, and its queasy banquet menu of chilled monkey brains isn't that far removed from Khan's favoured dish of stuffed sheep's head (please, help yourself to an eyeball...).

Octopussy's cinematic roots run deeper than the Jones boy, though. The safari hunt for Bond recalls 1932's *The Most Dangerous Game* while the fight on the roof of a thundering train feels like an homage to the earliest daredevilry of the screen.

BOND WARS

Octopussy is Roger Moore's sixth Bond caper – an unbroken run that equalled Connery's interrupted tally – but the renewal of his licence to kill was far from a formality. By now he was negotiating on a strictly film-by-film basis and, just like last time, his return was locked perilously late in the day.

Broccoli had a substitute 007 in mind: *The Amityville Horror*'s James Brolin, an American, whose screen test reveals a beef-flank of a Bond, incarnating Fleming's fastidious Etonian hero with what producer Michael G Wilson charitably called "a mid-Atlantic style."

Broccoli needed Moore, though. Alongside the thirteenth official Bond entry, 1983 would also see the release of *Never Say Never Again*, the long-threatened challenge to the franchise by rival producer Kevin McClory. Legally McClory could only rehash *Thunderball*, but he was armed with the screen rights to such iconic parts of Bond's heritage as Blofeld and SPECTRE, not to mention the ultimate intimidation of Sean Connery as his leading man, returning to secret service for the first time in 12 years. To many the 53 year old Scotsman endured as the once and future Bond and, as the press prepared to feast on the clash, Broccoli realised that *Octopussy* had to retaliate with the established star power of Roger Moore. His instincts were right: *Octopussy* outgrossed its ultimately underwhelming rival and Connery's return proved more of a footnote in film history than the second coming.

FULLY BOOKED

Once again the film-makers plundered Fleming's untapped short stories for inspiration. "Octopussy" had been published posthumously in 1966, a final attempt at milking the creator's canon for a Bond-hungry marketplace. Originally it gathered together two stories: the previously unpublished title tale and "The Living Daylights", written for The Sunday Times in 1962. The paperback added a third story, "The Property Of A Lady", penned by Fleming for The Ivory Hammer, the yearbook of Sotheby's auction house (neatly, we glimpse that title on the Sotheby's catalogue as Bond prepares to bid for the Fabergé egg in the movie). Told in flashback, Fleming's story is more morality tale than thriller, telling of 007's pursuit of disgraced military man Major Dexter Smythe, whose unlikely death by pet octopus is referenced in one of the movie's grislier, most pulpy moments.

"THAT'S MY LITTLE OCTOPUSSY"

Maud Adams is the first actress to have two bites of the Bond girl cherry (not counting Eunice Gayson's Sylvia Trench, whose encore in *From Russia With Love* is more of a cameo).

The Swedish-born former model played the ill-fated Andrea Anders in 1974's *The Man With The Golden Gun* and - 11 years after receiving Scaramanga's deftly delivered bullet in a Bangkok boxing stadium - returns as Octopussy herself, discreetly tattooed smuggler and queen of a kick-ass circus sisterhood.

It's revealed that she's the daughter of the doomed Major Smythe from Fleming's original short story. The film shuns the all too obvious revenge angle by having Octopussy thank Bond for allowing her father an honourable exit from the world.

Adams plays Octopussy with European allure but the filmmakers originally sought an East Indian actress for the part and briefly considered Persis Khambatta, best known for her strikingly bald turn as Lt Ilia in 1979's *Star Trek: The Motion Picture*. While Adams expressed reservations about the provocative name, she was happy to return to the Bond world: "Looking back on it, how can you not really enjoy the fact that you were a Bond girl? It's pop culture and to be part of that is very nice."

INDIAN SUMMER BLOCKBUSTER

Roger Moore suffered for his art on *Octopussy*. The star sweltered on location in India, forced to endlessly change shirts in a bid to preserve 007's unruffled image.

Tailoring crises aside, the subcontinent proves an intriguing new backdrop for Bond, accenting his origin as a post-colonial fantasy for a Britain struggling with the end of empire. The days of the Raj were an ongoing preoccupation for the country in the early '80s, one that chimed with a yearning for an imperial dream of a past that infiltrated everything from the fops and picnics of *Brideshead Revisited* to the jodhpurs of the New Romantics (future title song creators Duran Duran upheld the tradition of the well-heeled English traveller descending on the undeveloped world, blitzing Sri Lanka for a series of glossy promo vids). A year after *Octopussy* ITV would adapt Paul Scott's Raj-set novel *The Jewel In The Crown* to huge success, making a star of Art Malik, who would enter Bond's orbit in 1987's *The Living Daylights*.

More *Mind Your Language* than Midnight's Children, *Octopussy* is a cartoon notion of India, brimming with every reliable cliché from snake charmers to sword-swallowers to hot coals and beds of nails. Q's even perfecting the Indian Rope Trick.

CLOWNS, CAMP AND THE COLD WAR

113

Tonally, *Octopussy* is a distinctly strange entry in 007's big screen canon. *For Your Eyes Only* grounded Bond but only the ghost of that creative mission remains in its successor's Cold War concerns and glimpse of a cheerless East Berlin. Mention of mutual disarmament talks hint that the eternal Cold Warrior is rapidly edging towards a new world but elsewhere this is the Bond franchise at its campest: Octopussy's slave-boat feels like it's drifted in from a Sinbad flick while her personal island of harem-styled underlings is pure '30s Hollywood.

Not only is Roger Moore back in the faithful safari suit but the humour dial is heading remorselessly into the red again: Bond swings from a vine with an authentic Tarzan yell and stops a tiger with a topical nod to TV dog-wrangler Barbara Woodhouse. He even tells a snake to "Hiss off!" Ironically, what threatens to be the movie's daftest moment – Bond in clown suit, red nose and greasepaint, attempting to stop a warhead at a circus – becomes a brilliantly tense, quasi-Hitchcockian highlight.

Octopussy also brings some interesting new flavours to the mix. There's a marvellous echo of *The Avengers* in the early sequence where a clown and his balloon are chased by knife-throwing twins through a forest. The moment the clown crashes through the French windows of the British embassy and a Fabergé egg rolls from his dying hand is one of the greatest visual non-sequiturs in Bond history.

INTERCEPTED INTELLIGENCE

Steven Berkoff arrived for his audition as Orlov in a full samurai suit.

Faye Dunaway was in the frame for Octopussy while Barbara Carrera claimed that she turned down the role to star opposite Sean Connery in *Never Say Never Again*.

George MacDonald Fraser – author of the Flashman books – was brought in to develop the story and came up with the idea of the razor-edged yo-yo.

Moneypenny actress Lois Maxwell was dismayed by the presence of MI6 assistant Penelope Smallbone, who she imagined was being set up as her replacement.

The pre-credits stunt with the miniature jet was originally intended for *Moonraker*.

Stuntman Martin Grace spent six months in hospital after shattering his hip during the train sequence.

Vijay is played by Vijay Amritaj, real life professional tennis player (you can also glimpse him as a Starfleet captain in *Star Trek IV: The Voyage Home*).

Midge is played by former Pan's People dancer Cherry Gillespie.

A VIEW TO A KILL

1985 131 minutes

Director: John Glen

Writers: Michael G Wilson, Richard Maibaum

Score: John Barry

Title song: Duran Duran

Cast: Roger Moore, Tanya Roberts, Christopher Walken, Grace Jones, Patrick Macnee

A VIEW TO AN END

Roger Moore made the decision to renounce his double-0 status as production drew to a close on his seventh Bond film. He was 58. "I was only about 400 years too old for the part," he later recalled, with the twinkling self-deprecation he used as a pre-emptive strike against critics.

Technically, Moore was always just a tad too old for Bond. He had been 44 when *Live And Let Die* was released, 12 years older than Connery's debut in *Dr. No* and just one year shy of the mandatory retirement age for double-0 agents established by Ian Fleming in the pages of Moonraker.

While Moore's affable appeal remains unassailable, *A View To A Kill* is wounded by a creeping credibility gap between actor and character. By now audience and filmmakers are complicit in a kind of fantasy, a shared, unspoken joke that lets them reconcile long-shots of Bond performing Olympian-level skiing feats with close-ups of Moore in rear projection hell. Elsewhere careless editing betrays his stunt-double in the Paris car chase. Increasingly it's as if two entirely distinct universes are being cross-cut onscreen.

Moore's decision to leave 007 behind him had lasting consequences for his career. Unlike Connery he had never quite managed to parlay his status as Bond into true box office starpower and, a cameo in *Spice World* aside, *A View To A Kill* marks the last blockbuster on his long resume.

MAD MAX

Look closely and you'll see the ghost of David Bowie in genetically-modified madman Max Zorin.

Bowie's cultural stock was never higher than in the mid-'80s – shedding his earlier, edgier incarnations, the dancefloor-friendly beats of Let's Dance had seen him win a new mainstream audience and he'd earned critical acclaim for his performance in arthouse POW drama *Merry Christmas Mr Lawrence*. Eon wanted his alien glamour for the Bond

118

franchise but Bowie wasn't biting. "Absolutely out of the question," he told NME's Charles Shaar Murray. "I think for an actor it's probably an interesting thing to do, but I think that for somebody from rock it's more of a clown performance – and I didn't want to spend five months watching my double fall off mountains."

Brought to the screen with tripwire charisma by Christopher Walken, Max is an Aryan technocrat whose peroxide quiff and slick suits steal the media-conquering image Bowie created for his Serious Moonlight tour. Zorin is a quintessentially '80s villain, an unholy creation of Nazi superscience operating in the rapacious realm of big business. He demands "an exclusive marketing agreement" with his criminal collaborators and gleefully machine-guns his own workers – the ultimate filthy capitalist.

COMRADES IN CHARM

The notion that a 58 year old Roger Moore and a 63 year old Patrick Macnee are Britain's first line of defence is, to be honest, a whimsical one. 1985 is, after all, the year that Sylvester Stallone unleashed the vicious, steroidal *Rambo: First Blood Part Two* on the big screen, a movie that would adrenalise the Hollywood action flick.

But for all its hint of *Last Of The Summer Spies* there's a real frisson in this pairing of near-pensionable agents. Macnee won television immortality as the suave yet steely John Steed and the sight of him fighting alongside Bond feels like a genuine teaming of icons.

It was Barbara Broccoli who suggested Macnee for the role of MI6 operative Sir Godfrey Tibbett. He and Moore were old friends, spending the 1960s on adjoining Elstree soundstages as they conjured the competing escapist worlds of *The Avengers* and *The Saint* (Moore felt so comfortable in their friendship that he improvised extra jibes at Macnee's expense during filming). The veteran espionage star brings his dependable brand of barrel-aged charm to *A View To A Kill*, ensuring that Sir Godfrey's death feels like a personal loss for Bond and audience alike.

DANCE INTO THE FIRE

Duran Duran's title song arrives like a jolt of pure 1985. Now reborn as pastel-suited hedonists, the former New Romantics were a shrewd marketing choice on the part of the Bondmakers, a calculated grab for the Smash Hits demographic.

All Time High, Rita Coolidge's theme to *Octopussy*, had reached an ignominious number 75 on the British charts, the lowest ranking Bond song ever. A View To A Kill, by contrast, scored number one in the States and a creditable number two in the UK.

The band entered Bond's orbit after bassist John Taylor tipsily cornered Cubby Broccoli at a party and demanded "When are you going to get someone decent to do one of your theme songs?" They were on the verge of splintering into rival projects but just about contained their imminent implosion to deliver one of the last great Bond songs, an urgent, percussive pop-grenade that even elevates Simon Le Bon's usual parade of stream-of-consciousness MTV poetry into something elegant and lovely ("A chance to find the phoenix for the flame…").

Ironically, Duran Duran's image as model-chasing international playboys felt closer to the classic Bond dream than Roger Moore's increasingly leathery roué. As keyboardist Nick Rhodes recalled, "You had five people in the band who pretty much thought they were James Bond…"

STATE OF GRACE

Grace Jones occupies a unique place in 007 history – and not just for the insurrectionary moment she rolls on top of Bond in bed, seizing the dominant role in a reversal of the franchise's traditional sexual gameplay.

As the lethal May Day she's a perfect genetic splice between Bond girl and Bond hench, part Pussy Galore, part Jaws. She proved to be the key visual in the movie's marketing: "Has James Bond finally met his match?" demanded the poster campaign, placing Jones's half-naked Amazonian frame back to back with Roger Moore.

The Jamaican-born singer, actress and model had earned notoriety for slapping chat show king Russell Harty in an unforgettable display of black-gloved divadom. She brings a little of that livewire threat to Bond. There's something feral in the way she bites at Zorin before they kiss; you suspect her tumble in the sack with 007 must have been as demanding as any heart-stopping stunt sequence.

"SO, ANYONE ELSE WANT TO DROP OUT?"

A View To A Kill is the most vampiric of Bond movies. It feeds on youth, pitting its hero against a conspicuously younger generation of villains, injecting a shot of rock 'n' roll culture with Grace Jones and the Bowiesque Max Zorin and enlisting Duran Duran for a direct assault on the teenage heart.

But all its flashy, contemporary trappings cannot hide the fact that this once bulletproof franchise is feeling decidedly tired. The sight of Bond on skis in the pre-titles only reheats past glories, further undermined by a lousy cover of California

Girls surely lifted from one of those cut-price Beach Boys soundalike albums that infest motorway service stations.

Former *Charlie's Angels* star Tanya Roberts makes for a dull Bond girl, there's a deeply perfunctory fight in a warehouse, endless pottering around Zorin's stud farm and a chase with American cop cars that feels crushingly ordinary for 007. And for all that Bond impresses Stacey by baking her a quiche he's still cracking jokes about women's lib. Even Roger Moore knew that this was a film too far. Twenty three years after *Dr. No* the Bond franchise craved new blood like never before.

It was time to find the phoenix for the flame.

INTERCEPTED INTELLIGENCE:

The end credits of *Octopussy* announced "James Bond will return in *From A View To A Kill*", the original title of Fleming's short story.

After David Bowie turned down the role of Max Zorin the filmmakers attempted to woo Sting.

May Day's 960 ft leap from the Eiffel Tower was performed by BJ Worth. He had three seconds to clear the girders and used the sound of the wind in his ears as an altimeter. Producer

Michael G Wilson worked out the practicalities of the jump using calculus.

Full-size pieces of the Golden Gate bridge were replicated on the backlot at Pinewood.

An early version of the plot had Zorin attempting to alter the course of Halley's Comet.

Grace Jones's screams in the flooded mine are genuine. When the sparks went off she thought she was surrounded by live voltage.

The 007 Stage burnt down during Ridley Scott's filming of *Legend*. It was reopened on January 7th 1985 as the Albert R Broccoli 007 Stage.

Look for future *Rocky IV* and *Masters Of The Universe* star Dolph Lundgren as a KGB man. He was Grace Jones's boyfriend at the time.

THE LIVING DAYLIGHTS

1987 131 minutes

Director: John Glen

Writers: Richard Maibaum, Michael G Wilson

Score: John Barry

Title song: a-Ha

Cast: Timothy Dalton, Maryam d'Abo, Joe Don Baker, Jeroen Krabbé, Art Malik

BOND GOES FOURTH

After 14 years of secret service duty, the exit of Roger Moore left a tuxedo-clad void at the heart of the franchise.

The screenplay for the new Bond adventure was written with no leading man in mind. One early pitch favoured a total reset, exploring Bond's untold past, perhaps in a period setting. While the Bondmakers would eventually play the reboot card with 2006's *Casino Royale*, Cubby Broccoli vetoed this idea, arguing that 007 worked best as a seasoned agent with a legacy of sex and death on his scorecard.

As ever, every actor with a pulse and an Equity card appeared to be in consideration for the most coveted gig in cinema. *Robin Of Sherwood*'s mulleted bowman Michael Praed was one contender. So was *Reilly Ace Of Spies* star Sam Neill, who reportedly impressed everyone except Broccoli. On April 27 1986 The Mail On Sunday broke a "World Exclusive" – possibly bleeding into this reality from a parallel world – that named the fourth Bond as 32 year old Australian model Finley Light, supposedly signed for a 10 year stint in the spy game. "The Bond contract is pretty good," Light was quoted as saying. "I think it will work out for me."

Closer to reality, Broccoli had his eye on vulpine stage and screen actor Timothy Dalton, who he had courted for Bond ever since Connery bailed (Dalton refused that first advance, fearing he was too young). With Dalton committed elsewhere, Broccoli turned to a rising star named Pierce Brosnan, whose suave, knowing performance in American adventure series *Remington Steele* felt like one long screentest for Bond.

Brosnan's chance at big screen glory was crushed by an act of corporate mean-mindedness. Sensing he was a hot property, the network refused to release him, holding him to the letter of his contract. "My agents are going to make them pay," said Brosnan, who would wait nearly a decade to claim the role. "There's a lot of blood left to squeeze out of them."

As the schedule slipped, Dalton was suddenly available. The script was immediately tailored to his strengths. Dalton wanted Bond be the "tarnished man" of the Fleming novels, all of which he scrutinised with the instincts of a classical actor returning to the core text: "In the books you're dealing with a real man, not a superman, who is beset with moral confusions and apathies and uncertainties and who is often very frightened and nervous and tense. That has not come across in the films."

LIVING ON THE EDGE

Dalton walks the opening gunbarrel with an urgent, confident stride that declares a whole new slate for Bond.

More plausibly a flesh and blood secret servant than fantasy playboy, he substitutes intensity for Moore's impregnable charm, trades his predecessor's smirk for a snarl. For all his fine tailoring, his elegant way with a cigarette, there's a slowburn tension to his take, a sense of a man wounded by the psychological collateral of his job. Yes, occasionally he plays it like Heathcliff confronted by a particularly confounding tax return, and Bond's traditional one-liners tend to die unloved on his lips, but for all the petulant hint of a stick in his arse ("I'd rather not talk about it," he snaps) Dalton brings an authentic sense of inner life to Fleming's hero.

The film's marketing campaign sold us Dalton's aura of blade-eyed danger – "The most dangerous James Bond. Ever."

– and there's a vicious edge to his 007 that's never less than jolting. He strips a woman to distract a guard and when he commands Pushkin to kneel in preparation for a bullet in the head it feels uncomfortably close to the reality of state-sponsored execution. In that moment you're compelled to believe in this Bond's licence to kill.

BY WAY OF INTRODUCTION

The introduction of any new Bond is a cardinal moment and the pre-titles sequence of *The Living Daylights* wittily toys with our expectations.

We're flung into an MI6 training mission to penetrate the radar defences of Gibraltar. Three men skydive onto the towering, rain-grey crag of the crown dependency, a choice of location that declares a return to the grounded tone of *For Your Eyes Only*. One of these freefalling silhouettes is the new James Bond – but which one? The film is playing a shell game with Bond's identity.

When Dalton finally wins a close-up it's a beauty. He turns, a Byronic figure ruffled by high winds, all dimpled chin and sharp gaze as he processes the death-cry of a fellow double-0. As John Barry's score turns techno Bond enters white-knuckle action mode, battling to cling to an explosives-laden jeep as it careens around the perilous cliffside roads.

This combat-booted protagonist immediately feels more dynamic than Moore's incarnation. By the time he dispenses a brutal head-butt we're sold on him as an action man, a physical force. But Dalton's most telling moment comes when he introduces himself to the woman on the yacht. Confronted by the line "Bond, James Bond" he strips it of all its suave portent, its decades of encrusted meaning. He's like a Hamlet staring down theatrical history by tossing away "To be or not to be." The intent is clear: Timothy Dalton is playing James Bond. Just not the one we've always known.

THE MONOGAMOUS BOND

By 1987 James Bond was in danger of looking like a painfully archaic fantasy. A dream-figure of rapacious, all-conquering male desire, the character seemed inseparable from the sexual revolution of the 1960s, licenced to bed the planet as often as he saved it.

But now came the media-ordained era of Safe Sex. The threat of AIDS was impacting on society and there was an unshakable suspicion that the '60s party was finally at an end. While the filmmakers denied that this new moral code infiltrated *The Living Daylights* it's clear that Dalton is being repositioned as a more monogamous figure. His pre-titles dalliance on the yacht aside, this Bond is a one-woman man, and the film ultimately delivers the most credible romance since *On Her Majesty's Secret Service*.

Dalton is the first and only actor to imagine Bond as a true romantic lead. He had played Heathcliff and Rochester and brings a little of that matinee idol smoulder to 007, always holding the girl's head in his hands as he moves to kiss her. Crucially, he never feels like a player. "I heard you played the conservatoire yesterday," he tells Kara, the cellist ensnared in this adventure. "It was exquisite." With any other Bond that might seem like a line. With Dalton it feels like a flash of a buried heart, a glimpse of a sensitive man grasping for beauty in a bruising world.

OPTIONAL EXTRAS

While Roger Moore was synonymous with the sleek Lotus Esprit - in both submersible and turbo-charged versions - Bond's back behind the wheel of an Aston Martin in *The Living Daylights*. The iconic choice of marque was a calculated one by the filmmakers, keen to arm their new Bond with a sense of big screen heritage.

Dalton drives an Aston Martin V8 Volante, first seen as a convertible and then craftily "winterised" into a hard-top by Q Branch. The car packs hubcap-mounted lasers, heat-seeking missiles and an internal HUD display; retractable outriggers and tyre-spikes allow it to outwit icy weather. All of this is, of course, deeply satisfying for your inner ten year old but it feels just a little jarring in this Bond film, with its emphasis on grounded adventure and Cold War spygaming.

Dalton clearly struggles with the Mooreisms – "I had a few optional extras installed," he mutters, barely summoning a twinkle – and by the time a roaring jet-flame erupts from the rear of the Aston it's as if the Batmobile has crashed headlong into *Tinker, Tailor, Soldier, Spy*.

SMERT SPIONEM

The Living Daylights takes the premise of Fleming's original 1962 short story – a melancholy 007 encounters a lady cellist assassin and deliberately fudges his assigned kill – and uses it as the catalyst for a mazy tale of deceptions and double-crosses.

Notably it's the last Cold War Bond adventure. We're in the dying days of the shadow-conflict that powered *From Russia With Love* and deeper into the game than ever before. The rain-slick cobbles and seedy, watchful back rooms of Bratislava conjure the authentic atmosphere of a John Le Carré tale or some other gloomy spy thriller. We wouldn't be entirely surprised if Callan, Smiley or Harry Palmer were on the other side of the walls, peering into the Czechoslovakian darkness, listening to the secret chatter of spooks in the night.

Elsewhere the film's Viennese sequences nod to Carol Reed's classic 1949 film noir *The Third Man* – director John Glen had started his career as assistant to the sound department on that film, and wanted to pay tribute – while the climax in Afghanistan delivers a romantic desert adventure vibe, as epic and widescreen as the earlier Cold War manoeuverings are boxy and internal. Art Malik's turn as the heroic, charismatic leader of the Afghan rebels, meanwhile, is now very much a snapshot of a pre-9/11 world.

INTERCEPTED INTELLIGENCE

Other contenders for Bond included Lambert Wilson, Anthony Hamilton and Christopher Lambert, star of *Highlander*.

Maryam d'Abo helped screentest the potential Bonds. She had originally auditioned for the role of Pola Ivanova in A View To A Kill, a role that was won by Fiona Fullerton.

Ian Fleming's original title for "The Living Daylights" was "Trigger Finger".

A scene deleted from the film finds Bond riding a "flying carpet" above the souks of Morocco. It was deleted for being a little too Roger Moore in tone.

Dalton began his Bond career in a state of jet-lag. He finished *Brenda Starr* in America on a Saturday, flew Sunday and began filming *The Living Daylights* on the Monday.

Andreas Wisniewski AKA Walkman-wielding assassin Necros was a trained ballet dancer.

This is the last film to be scored by John Barry. He cameos as the conductor of the orchestra as Kara plays.

LICENCE TO KILL

1989 133 minutes

Director: John Glen

Writers: Michael G Wilson, Richard Maibaum

Score: Michael Kamen

Title song: Gladys Knight

Cast: Timothy Dalton, Carey Lowell, Robert Davi, Talisa Soto, Anthony Zerbe

TRY HARD WITH A VENGEANCE

The sixteenth Bond film has blood on its knuckles. The most vicious-hearted of all 007's adventures, it puts a final bullet in the lingering ghost of the Roger Moore years.

Emboldened by the success of the harder-edged *The Living Daylights*, Dalton and director John Glen pushed for an even more bruising take on Fleming's hero, one that refused to blink at the inescapable violence of Bond's world.

The movie's cruel streak is clear from the opening scenes. While the duplicitous villains of *Daylights* had been the feeblest in the franchise's history, cocaine kingpin Franz Sanchez makes an instant, censor-baiting impact. Confronted by a cheating moll, he orders the heart of her lover hacked out and then presents it to her as the ultimate bloody valentine before taking a whip to her body. Fleming's taste for a little light S&M frequently infiltrated the original novels but the brutality of this sequence has none of his characteristic kinky quiver (a torture scene with a similar dynamic in Thunderball plays out with far more dark imagination).

Savage tone duly established, the movie relentlessly jabs at the acceptable limits of big screen Bond. When a crooked DEA agent slams a rifle butt into a man's face there's a shocking bloom of blood; elsewhere the nefarious Milton Krest explodes inside a pressure chamber, blotching a window with brain-jam. "Bond exists in a violent world and has to use violence against violence," declared Dalton, unapologetically.

For all that it pursues adult sensibilities there's a touch of try-hard about this blood-letting, and it's telling that this is also the first truly sweary Bond movie: 007 himself tells an MI6 colleague to "Piss off", an uncharacteristically raw moment that punctures decades' worth of nonchalant cool.

Licence To Kill earned a 15 certificate on release in the UK, the first Bond film to be exiled from a traditional family audience.

THIS TIME IT'S PERSONAL

Trading Whitehall-sanctioned world-saving for a personal vendetta, *Licence To Kill* repositions 007 as a late '80s action hero: a self-motivated force for hi-octane redemption, operating distinctly off the grid.

This is the age of *Rambo*, *Commando* and *Die Hard*, after all, but there's also a belated echo of *Dirty Harry* and *Death Wish* in Bond's newfound disdain for authority and his embracing of lone wolf status. Stylistically the shadow of *Miami Vice* looms large: Michael Mann's cop drama had recently redefined TV detective shows and here Bond invades its drug war turf without ever quite capturing its slick, cocaine-benumbed '80s sheen (they even enlisted the show's costume designer, Jodie Tillen). The ruthless, reptillian Sanchez could easily have faced Crockett and Tubbs on the small screen, but inspiration for the movie's villain was in fact found in real life. Demanding an antagonist "ripped from the headlines", the screenwriters channelled the true life evil of Manuel Noriega, the Panamanian drug king whose leathery, pitted countenance is clearly mirrored in Robert Davi's casting.

DALTON TAKE TWO

Who exactly is Timothy Dalton playing in *Licence To Kill*? It's sold to us as a James Bond film but its gruff hero bears scant resemblance to the cinematic archetype established by Connery and Moore. If his predecessors had occasionally felt like suave, untouchable holograms, dancing through glamorous peril with the easy confidence of those who are born bulletproof, then Dalton is the first Bond to bleed persuasively.

He gives a strikingly less charming performance in this film. While *The Living Daylights* had shown us a 007 whose romantic side softened his steel, this vengeance-fuelled version is an altogether different proposition, a brusque, ill-tempered bastard with a gaze like a furnace. He simmers as M revokes his licence to kill, threatens Lupe with a blade to her throat. Sacrificing a corrupt DEA agent to a shark his face remains impassive and not a little scary. He's almost fed into a giant shredder in Sanchez' cocaine plant: "Switch the bloody machine off!" he barks, trading Bond's usual cool disdain for the very real reaction of a man who's a heartbeat from a grisly death ("Do you expect me to talk, Goldfinger?" feels a universe away). Even his delivery of signature line "Shaken not stirred" is weirdly brutal, closer to a punch than a smile.

Dalton's never less than compelling, though, and his sheer acting chops let us buy into this wounded, human Bond, which in turn sells the vendetta that drives the plot. When he discovers the body of Felix's murdered wife his anguished cry of "Della!" is genuinely jolting. Seconds later, you clearly see that a fuse has been lit, one that will burn all the way to Mexico's Isthmus City and Franz Sanchez, trailing blood, bullets and fire.

A GENUINE FELIX LEITER

Bond seeks revenge on behalf of Felix Leiter, his old CIA contact and possibly the closest this most self-reliant of heroes has to a friend.

Ian Fleming introduces 007's Stateside ally in the very first Bond novel, Casino Royale, "a cool and quiet no-nonsense character who knows 007's strengths and weaknesses well". Future *Hawaii Five-0* icon Jack Lord established the big screen Felix in *Dr. No* but never returned to the role – some say he demanded too much money to come back, others believe the filmmakers feared that Lord's towering, sharp-suited cool threatened to eclipse their star. The compulsively recast Leiters who pop up in *Goldfinger*, *Thunderball* and *Diamonds Are Forever* certainly possess a fraction of Lord's charisma and feel far from rivals to Bond's alpha male status (only *Thunderball*'s Rik Van Nutter lodges in the memory, and that's mainly for his name).

While *The Living Daylights* had introduced yet another forgettable Felix in John Terry, Broccoli argued that for *Licence To Kill*'s story to have any resonance it needed an actor who had a history with the Bond franchise. Time to recall David Hedison, Roger Moore's co-star in 1973's *Live And Let Die*. Director John Glen initially thought that, at 62, Hedison was too old to be a convincing compatriot of the fortysomething Dalton and, in truth, he's a perplexing choice, looking more like a freshly reupholstered morning show host than CIA badass. Even more perplexingly, the end of the movie finds him cosily joshing with Bond about an upcoming fishing vacation – not the most appropriate moment for a man who's just survived a mauling by a Great White, let alone one whose wife was raped and murdered on their wedding day.

TANKING CRISIS

Licence To Kill's centrepiece action scene finds Bond at the wheel of a tanker, manoeuvering its long, gleaming bulk through tortuous Mexican mountain roads filled with dust and fireballs and the chatter of machine gun fire.

There's a muscular Monster Truck Show vibe to this stunt sequence, never more so than in the moment the tanker performs a gravity-mocking wheelie. Kenworth Trucks fitted a 1000 horsepower engine, close to three times the amount of horsepower on a normal tanker; five tons of weight were also placed over the back wheels so it could attempt the feat.

Filming took place at the La Rumorosa Mountain Pass in Mexicali and required a total of 16 18-wheeler trucks, corralled by veteran stunt co-ordinator Remy Julienne, who performed the astonishing tanker-tilt without recourse to a special rig that had been constructed for the shot.

LICENCE REVOKED

Ultimately *Licence To Kill* feels like a tussle for the soul of Bond. It chases a place at the high table of '80s action flicks but it's in danger of bartering the franchise's special magic for the kind of mundane, low-horizon thrills you can find in any Chuck Norris VHSer.

On release in 1989 it notably failed to find an audience in the States, crushed by a blockbuster summer that included such multiplex-fillers as *Batman*, *Lethal Weapon 2* and *Indiana Jones And The Last Crusade* (Bond has never dared step into the summer arena since). It was also crippled by a lacklustre marketing campaign: gone were the traditional painted posters with their high-end glamour, replaced by drab photo montages that made a point of ditching Bond's time-honoured tux.

Cubby Broccoli soon realised that this surly, single-minded new Bond was a misstep. "In making Bond an altogether tougher character we had lost some of the original sophistication and wry humour," he confessed in his 1998 autobiography When The Snow Melts. "Bond is not a Superman, or a Rambo... He is, as Fleming insisted, a skilled professional: ruthless and sardonic in his work; gentle, witty and stylish off duty. That is the way the public want him and it's clear we had to get back on to that track."

As tired as it's revolutionary, lumbered with the dullest title in the series, *Licence To Kill* closes a chapter on James Bond in the cinema. It would be a long six years before Her Majesty's secret servant returned to the screen, and in that time he would shed familiar names from both in front of and behind the camera. Perhaps sensing his licence to kill would soon be lost, Timothy Dalton went bluntly off-brand when he told a journalist "My feeling is this will be the last one. I don't mean my last one. I mean the end of the whole lot. I don't speak with any real authority, but it's a feeling I have. Sorry!"

But as that invincible mantra always tell us, James Bond will return…

INTERCEPTED INTELLIGENCE

China was the original choice of location for this adventure. Potential story elements included a motorbike chase along the Great Wall and a fight sequence among the priceless Terracotta Army.

The film uses two unfilmed ideas from Ian Fleming's original Live And Let Die – Felix's shark torture and Milton Krest's fish factory.

Originally titled *Licence Revoked*, the movie was renamed after the studio fretted that the word revoked would be a hard sell in the US.

A key influence was Akira Kurosawa's classic revenge tale *Yojimbo*.

MGM refused to run a series of stylish teaser posters by *The Spy Who Loved Me* billboard artist Bob Peak, much to Broccoli's annoyance.

Robert Davi played Bond in the screentests for Lupe.

President Lopez is played by the son of Pedro Armendáriz, who played Bond's ally Kerim Bey in *From Russia With Love*.

GOLDENEYE

1995 130 minutes

Director: Martin Campbell

Writers: Jeffrey Caine, Bruce Feirstein, Michael France, Kevin Wade

Score: Eric Serra

Title song: Tina Turner

Cast: Pierce Brosnan, Izabella Scorupco, Sean Bean, Famke Janssen, Judi Dench

NO LIMITS. NO FEARS. NO SUBSTITUTES

"You know the name. You know the number" asserted the teaser poster to *GoldenEye*, summoning all the cocksure confidence of the James Bond brand.

It was an essential show of bravado. By 1995 007 was staring down an enemy greater than the combined might of SPECTRE and SMERSH – cultural irrelevance. It had been six years since the underperforming *Licence To Kill*, a lifetime for a franchise machine accustomed to box office strikes on a strict two-year basis.

The filmmakers had been locked in a legal brawl with a financially bruised MGM and while the early '90s saw murmurs of a new Bond adventure – a more SF-tinged escapade, pitting Dalton's grounded man-of-action against hi-tech robots – the once world-owning phenomenon seemed closer than ever to sputtering into obsolescence.

Cubby Broccoli for one feared that Bond's stock was in freefall. He filed suit against MGM after the studio attempted to sell the films at giveaway prices to foreign TV and video markets. You can understand the old showman's alarm – Fleming's hero traded in gilt-edged dreams, not bargain basement offers. By 1995 the superspy not only needed to reclaim his place in pop culture – he had to rebuild his own brand. The world knew the name, the world knew the number. Crucially, did it still care?

"I WATCHED YOU FROM THE SHADOWS AS A CHILD"

"When it came around again, I didn't think twice," declared Pierce Brosnan, the fifth actor to earn the cinematic licence to kill. "It was unfinished business." In 1986 he had famously lost the role to Dalton over a contractual wrangle and while there was no shortage of pretender Bonds touted by the tabloids – everyone from Mel Gibson to Liam Neeson and Hugh Grant –

Brosnan's appointment felt ordained, inevitable, the people's choice.

Revealed to the world's press on 7th June 1994, the Irish-born actor spoke of a lifelong enchantment with Bond's impossible universe. He was the first star of the franchise to have experienced its impact as a kid: "When I was 11 I came to London with a bottle of water in one hand and my rosary in the other, and the first movie I saw was *Goldfinger*. I looked up at the big screen for the first time and I saw a naked lady and a cool man who could get out of any situation. I was captivated, magicked, blown away."

Look closely and you can see the ghost of that bedazzled little boy in Brosnan's Bond. It's there in his grin as he guns a gleaming Aston Martin around the hairpin roads of Monaco; it echoes in his twinkle as he moves through the glamour of Monte Carlo, more naturally at home in a tuxedo than Dalton ever was, dusting his entendres with irony in that soft Irish brogue. He's playing James Bond, but he's also playing at being James Bond. And yet there's more to Brosnan than dimpled charm and breathy innuendo. He vowed to make Bond "human and real and accessible", and *GoldenEye* makes it a mission to tease out the character's shadows. "How can you be so cold?" asks Natalya, confronted by 007's emotional armour. "It's what keeps me alive," answers Bond, an admission that feels as much a wound as a weapon.

JUMP!

It's the breathtaking stunt that declares Bond's inimitable return to the big screen: a freefall bungee jump into the granite vastness of the Arkangel chemical weapons facility. As *GoldenEye* opens a black-clad 007 executes a graceful swan dive into its seemingly infinite maw, clearly in danger of being smashed to pulp by its blind grey walls.

Switzerland's virtually vertical Locarno dam delivered the backdrop while Wayne Michaels doubled for Brosnan on the daredevil leap, a 700 ft plummet that was nailed in one take and set a new world record (Michaels recalled that he saw an Italian crane driver make the sign of the cross before he jumped). A showcase for the Bond tradition of risk-taking stuntwork in an increasingly digital age, this leap launches the seventeenth Bond adventure in audacious style.

NEW WORLD DISORDER

"The map had changed," said director Martin Campbell, acknowledging that 007's resurrection was occurring in a radically transformed world. "Russia had changed, the whole political spectrum had changed – Bond has adapted."

The decades-long powerplay between East and West had been the background hum of Bond's big screen career. In his absence from active duty the Cold War had finally defrosted. New title designer Danny Kleinman's astonishing credits form the franchise's belated response to the fall of the USSR: golden girls writhe against blood-red clouds as sinister, sky-high supermodels take pick-axes to Soviet icons. Statues of Lenin and Marx topple like abandoned ideology. It feels like the final triumph of moneyed Western decadence, communism crushed beneath the power of the stiletto heel, collectivism assassinated by glamour.

By the time Bond re-enters history the New World Order of 1989 has soured. Crime has filled the vacuum left by the old orthodoxy and broken effigies of socialist heroes now decorate a junkyard, looming spectrally in the night. Tellingly, the villainous Alec Trevelyan wields a Cold War weapon, an electro-magnetic pulse that targets Britain's financial district. It may be a new world but Bond is still battling old ghosts.

FAMKE FATALE

From *Thunderball*'s Fiona Volpe to *A View To A Kill*'s May Day, the Bad Bond Girl is an infrequent but familiar player in the franchise. *GoldenEye*'s Xenia Onatopp takes the archetype to memorable new extremes. Clamping an oversized cigar between her teeth in a manner to make Freud blush, she just about steals the movie – sex-fighting with Bond in a sauna, writhing ferally on top of a doomed lover and panting orgasmically as she unleashes round after round of machine gun fire as if on some libidinous kill-spree. She's brought to the screen by Dutch ex-model Famke Janssen, who declared "I've deliberately gone to Cruella de Vil glam extremes and made her one sick bitch. I can't play housewives or girlfriend parts because of the way I look. So I've become the ultimate villainess instead."

"JAMES, YOU'RE INCORRIGIBLE!"

Was there still a place for James Bond in the '90s? Smartly, *GoldenEye* places this burning question centrestage. And then souses it with gasoline, just for good measure.

Judi Dench's new M denounces Bond as "a sexist, misogynist dinosaur, a relic of the Cold War", and these words feel like a pre-emptive strike, as if the film itself is finding a voice for its potential critics. She's not alone. "You know, this sort of behaviour could qualify as sexual harassment," reproaches Samantha Bond's Moneypenny, whose flirtation with 007 is notably flintier than her predecessors'. Elsewhere the movie takes sly jabs at our hero's rep: "James Bond, charming, sophisticated secret agent, shaken but not stirred," ribs Zukovsky, triggering laughter from his men. Bond's old fashioned sense of obligation to Queen and country finds him branded "Her Majesty's loyal terrier" while the treacherous 006 pointedly says "I might as well ask you if all those vodka martinis ever silence the screams of the men you've killed." It's as if every last character in the film is a critic, articulating some long-simmering agenda against its protagonist.

But timing was on Bond's side. Far from a cobwebbed relic he returned to '90s Britain as a conquering hero, a reclaimed icon for the age of Britpop (notably, a model in the title song's promo video wraps herself in a Union Jack, anticipating New Labour's Cool Britannia and a flag-draped Geri Halliwell). This was a land where the monochrome shark-gaze of Michael Caine in his '60s prime conferred instant cred on the covers of men's monthlies, where Easy Listening compilations conjured a notion of tight-suited bachelor cool soundtracked by the majestic swoon of John Barry.

Even Bond's unreconstructed sexual politics seemed in synch with the times. The beery rise of Loaded magazine had seen the emergence of the New Lad – Bond's strikingly uncharacteristic "Buy me a pint!" feels like a nod to this phenomenon – and a pseudo-ironic backlash against the buttoned-down '80s saw the return of pin-up culture and an unashamed celebration of the *Carry On* mindset. "I like a woman who enjoys pulling rank," declares Bond, trading a rapidfire volley of double entendres with Xenia – and the knowing, postmodern '90s audience is smirking too. For all that the film playfully pricks its own mythology, James Bond is hugely at home in 1995, the reissued *Goldfinger* score in his CD player, Jo Guest in his arms.

INTERCEPTED INTELLIGENCE

Director Martin Campbell spotted Famke Janssen in the rushes of Clive Barker's *Lord Of Illusions*.

For the city-smashing tank chase production designer Peter Lamont recreated St Petersburg on the backlot of Leavesden studios. It took 175 workmen over six weeks to create two acres of makebelieve Russia.

Sean Bean was in contention for the role of Bond himself.

After *GoldenEye*'s release the Locarno dam was leased by a commercial bungee jump operator for particularly brave thrill-seekers.

Goldeneye was the name of Ian Fleming's bolthole in Jamaica, the home where he wrote the Bond novels. It's also the name of a 1989 Fleming bio-pic that starred Charles Dance as Bond's creator.

GoldenEye sees the first mention of the Internet in the Bond films. And email. And the word geek.

TOMORROW NEVER DIES

1997 119 minutes

Director: Roger Spottiswoode

Writers: Bruce Feirstein, Nicholas Meyer, Daniel Petrie Jr

Score: David Arnold

Title song: Sheryl Crowe

Cast: Pierce Brosnan, Michelle Yeoh, Jonathan Pryce, Teri Hatcher, Joe Don Baker

BRAVE NEWS WORLD

As James Bond edged towards the 21st Century so, inevitably, did his adversaries. *Tomorrow Never Dies* submits a suitably pre-Millennial threat in the form of publishing czar Elliot Carver, a "worldwide media baron, able to topple governments with a single broadcast."

Carver's goal may be one of the more esoteric in the icy canon of Bond villainy - he craves exclusive Chinese broadcasting rights for the next 100 years, a demand that would surely summon a disdainful sneer from Blofeld or Stromberg – but he's a fitting foe for the age. The '90s had seen the rise of 24/7 news media, a rapacious arena that duelled in spectacle and soundbites, turning everything from the Gulf War to the OJ Simpson murder trial into intravenous infotainment for the masses. "Words are the new weapons, satellites are the new artillery," pitched screenwriter Bruce Feirstein, a clever line he relished so much it made its way into the movie.

A monstrous amalgam of Rupert Murdoch, Robert Maxwell and Steve Jobs, Carver is brought to snide, thin-lipped life by Jonathan Pryce. "I'm having fun with my headlines!" he declares, the electric glow of reflected newstype filling his frameless spectacles. For all that Carver's ambitions brought a topical hum, *Tomorrow Never Dies* now plays as a period piece. As his crooked newspaper thunders through the printing presses, we know that a real world phenomenon named the internet will soon unseat his empire of ink.

YEOH, BABY

By now the words "She's not the typical Bond girl" are an obligatory part of any press junket, as much a cliché as the bikini-clad notion of spy-candy they try to bury. With Michelle Yeoh, however, we finally buy it.

The Eastern cinema star brings a lethal self-possession to the role of Wai Lin, agent of the Chinese People's External Security Force and an unusually persuasive attempt on the part of the producers to forge a true female counterpart to 007. If

153

there's a touch of the Emma Peels about her it's by design – the cat-suited *Avengers* icon directly inspired her costume, along with Honor Blackman's imperial dominatrix Cathy Gale. More vitally, Wai Lin wears the influence of Asian action flicks, a screen phenomenon that was now cross-pollinating with Western cinema, enshrining Jackie Chan and John Woo as marquee names and whose flashy, kinetic energy would soon propel *The Matrix*.

Yeoh's casting may have been a calculated bid to court Eastern box office – she'd already earned stardom in such early '90s martial artsers as *Police Story 3: Super Cop* – but as a female lead in a Bond film she's a revolution. "I work alone," she tells 007, and for once you suspect Fleming's superspy may just have strayed into another action hero's franchise.

"ALL THE USUAL REFINEMENTS"

We glimpse Bond's silver DB5 in *Tomorrow Never Dies* but Q Branch soon delivers a distinctly less patriotic set of wheels – the BMW 750iL. There's just a hint of discreetly moneyed Dusseldorf dentist in the choice – and the sight of Bond driving a car with four doors is inexplicably jarring – but at least it packs all the optional extras tradition demands (*GoldenEye* had talked up a gadget-laden BMW Z3, only to cheat us when it came to a display of its arsenal).

The 750iL incorporates enough tech to sink the heart of an MI6 bean-counter: sunroof-mounted rockets, magnetic grenades, re-inflating tyres, chain-cutter, spike dispenser, tear gas, high-voltage defence system and bulletproof glass. Brilliantly it's also commanded by remote control. Just watch as Bond's face cracks into a boyish grin as he directs the car from the back seat. He may have discovered the corpse of a murdered lover only moments before but Q's latest toy lets him retreat to the place where nothing touches him, nothing but the adrenalinised delight of playing secret agent. Once again we catch sight of the thrilled kid inside Brosnan's slick, Brioni-suited Bond.

THE BIKE CHASE

It's the most knuckle-tightening action sequence in *Tomorrow Never Dies* – handcuffed together, Bond and Wai Lin gun a motorcycle through the slums of Saigon, strafed by the whip-blur blades of a pursuing helicopter. The bickering agents rocket the bike between two buildings, vaulting the chopper itself, a piece of daredevil showmanship performed by Jean Pierre Goy, who would go on to ride the Bat-pod in *The Dark Knight*.

"A lot of things could have gone wrong," recalled Goy, who refused a safety wire for the feat after a punishing 200 practice jumps. "I could have miscalculated the speed, the angle, the deviation from wind factors... the heat of the engine and exhausts could have set the cartons where I was landing in flames." True to Bond tradition, Goy executed the stunt in one immaculate, heart-stopping take.

KEEPING SCORE

The producers wanted John Barry's signature magic to soundtrack *Tomorrow Never Dies*. The veteran composer had recently found himself deified by retro-minded scenesters – the Pulp track This Is Hardcore, for instance, added a glassy *Ipcress File* melancholy to a typical Jarvis tale of broken suburban sexuality. Elsewhere everyone from Bjork to Catatonia set out to steal a shimmer of '60s cool. What better moment for the master himself to return? Barry refused the assignment but recommended a young composer named David Arnold, who would become a key player in the franchise as Bond met the Millennium. Crucially, Arnold was a fan. His love of the films had seen him create Shaken And Stirred: The David Arnold James Bond Project, an album of title anthems performed by such names as Iggy Pop and the Propellerheads.

The fan impulse was a new component in the creative mix of a Bond movie and it lends the score of *Tomorrow Never Dies* a self-referential quality, from the vintage strut that

156

accompanies the gunbarrel sequence to the knowing quotes from Barry's score to *From Russia With Love*.

POWERS STRUGGLE

David Arnold's soundtrack isn't the only element of *Tomorrow Never Dies* conjuring the ghosts of classic Bond. Even more than *GoldenEye* it feels like the first truly postmodern 007 adventure, a typical piece of mid '90s pop culture that synthesises iconic fragments of the past into a half-ironic, half-worshipful whole. Think Britpop, think Tarantino.

The sinking of the HMS Devonshire in the South China Seas echoes similar scenes in *The Spy Who Loved Me* and *For Your Eyes Only*. Carver's henchman Mr Stamper is in the Aryan bully boy mould of *From Russia With Love*'s Red Grant, *You Only Live Twice*'s Hans and Necros from *The Living Daylights*. Carver himself clearly shops at the designer fashion outlet favoured by archetypal Bond villains ("Perhaps sir would like this in world-threatening black? It's very slimming…"). Brosnan's investigation of the submerged Devonshire recalls Connery's exploration of the fallen Vulcans in *Thunderball* while Jack Wade, Bond's new CIA contact, splices Felix Leiter with the fat-mouthed comedy of Sheriff J W Pepper.

From the mandatory Aston Martin appearance to k d lang's Bassey-pastiche of an end credits song, *Tomorrow Never Dies* is a pick 'n' mix of Bond DNA. If it's all ultimately played with a respectful, oh so '90s wink then a new big screen rival wouldn't be so kind. The summer of 1997 saw the arrival of *Austin Powers*, Mike Myers's snaggle-toothed, velvet-suited skewering of the entire Bond phenomenon. 007 had outrun spoofs before, of course, but this strike was nuclear. Dr Evil alone ensured that Blofeld or any other Nehru-suited, globe-extorting mastermind wouldn't be troubling the franchise any time soon.

From this moment on the plots are (with one notable exception) dialed back, the elements that evoke Bond's traditional sense of macabre camp extracted. *Tomorrow Never Dies* would be the last Bond film to exist in a state of innocence. *Austin Powers* shook 007's confidence in his own extraordinary, gloriously implausible universe.

INTERCEPTED INTELLIGENCE

Tomorrow Never Dies was to be filmed on location in Vietnam, but the filmmakers couldn't secure permission.

The producers wooed *GoldenEye* director Martin Campbell. He refused, not wanting to do two Bond films in a row. He would return to launch Daniel Craig in 2006's *Casino Royale*.

The film's villain was originally named Elliot Harmsway. Anthony Hopkins was reportedly first choice for the role.

The film is dedicated to Albert R 'Cubby' Broccoli, who passed away before production began.

Tomorrow Never Dies is the first title not to have a direct connection to Ian Fleming. The movie was originally titled *Tomorrow Never Lies* – a reference to Carver's newspaper of that name – but a miscommunicated fax apparently rechristened it.

Any British act with a record contract appeared to be in competition for the coveted title song, from Pulp to Saint Etienne to Dot Allison. Pulp released their song, Tomorrow Never Lies, as the B-side to Help The Aged.

THE WORLD IS NOT ENOUGH

1999 125 minutes

Director: Michael Apted

Writers: Neal Purvis, Robert Wade, Bruce Feirstein

Score: David Arnold

Title song: Garbage

Cast: Pierce Brosnan, Sophie Marceau, Robert Carlyle, Denise Richards, Robbie Coltrane

APTED CHOICE

Watch the gunbarrel sequence that launches the last Bond film of the 20th Century. As Pierce Brosnan walks that familiar blank circle of infinite promise, David Arnold scores our hero's signature theme with a shiny techno edge. It's the sound of smoothly grinding metal, suggesting a reborn franchise nearing the Millennium as a perfectly calibrated piece of screen machinery. The truth was a little different.

Crippled by a troubled production and a script that seemed to exist in a state of quantum flux, *Tomorrow Never Dies* had ultimately dismayed its makers: too much clatter, they thought, too many blazing machine guns. They were determined to redress the balance with Bond's nineteenth adventure, arming their new movie with heart and emotional muscle. Key to this mission was the choice of Michael Apted as director, perhaps the most left-field pick in Bond history.

There was nothing on Apted's showreel that suggested an affinity for the traditional glitter and poison of Fleming's world. He had made a name for himself as a socially-minded documentary maker with the *7 Up* series; the closest he had strayed to Bond territory were such low-key thrillers as *Gorky Park* and *Extreme Measures*. "What was I doing directing a Bond film?" he recalls asking, intimidated by both the practical demands of a top-flight action franchise and the sheer scale of the phenomenon he was now entrusted with. He was especially unnerved by the crowds watching the shoot in Bilbao – in that moment, he said, the idea of the audience became both tangible and terrifying.

But Apted had a reputation for conjuring the best from his female leads in such fare as *The Coal Miner's Daughter* and *Gorillas In The Mist*. And, crucially, *The World Is Not Enough* would showcase the franchise's first true supervillainess, in a tale that would satisfy its star's craving for "complexity and depth." "Michael, give me stuff to do," begged Brosnan, forever wary of Bond's descent into Action Mannequin mode. "Give me scenes to play."

MOURNING BECOMES ELEKTRA

Ian Fleming's heroines were often wounded creatures. Elektra King, the treacherous oil heiress at the heart of *The World Is Not Enough*, is the ultimate "bird with a broken wing". She's scarred both physically and psychologically. Kidnapped as a teenager by the terrorist Renard, she fell in love with her abductor while developing serious daddy issues over her tycoon father's refusal to pay the ransom. Bond accuses her of Stockholm Syndrome but Elektra accuses him of using her as bait to snare Renard. These are unusually layered character beats for a Bond villain – we certainly never glimpsed Hugo Drax on the psychiatrist's couch, rationalising his space shuttle obsession as some deep-rooted phallic insecurity.

Elektra's scheme to contaminate the Bosphorous and force everyone to use her oil may be torn straight from the *Goldfinger* playbook but French cinema star Sophie Marceau makes this splintered beauty one of the more intriguing propositions in the pantheon of Bond villainy.

GOODBYE, Q

The World Is Not Enough proves a swansong for MI6's tweedy sorcerer. Arming 007 since 1963, Desmond Llewellyn's familiar note of sweet exasperation provided a crucial cord of continuity between all five Bond eras – and earned a place in the national heart, his fussy but boyish gadget demos as welcome as Christmas.

"You're not retiring any time soon, are you?" asks Bond, as he meets Q's new assistant (John Cleese, playing it like Basil Fawlty with an advanced engineering degree). We share 007's clear concern. Llewellyn was a snowy 85 now, but so embedded in the Bond myth that the thought of his absence was as inconceivable as the ravens fleeing the Tower of London.

"I've always tried to teach you two things," says the cantankerous tech-master. "First never let them see you bleed." And the second? "Always have an escape plan." Perhaps you hear the screenwriters trying just a little too hard here: Q's certainly never traded in that kind of Sandhurst wisdom. But no matter. Accompanied by a sombre musical cue, Q's final, wordless descent out of shot is a supremely poignant moment. Llewellyn died in a car crash less than a month after the London premiere.

TALES FROM THE RIVERBANK

The World Is Not Enough is front-loaded with one of the franchise's most thrilling extended action sequences. Launching Q's prototype jet-boat like a sleek grey dart, Bond smashes into the cold Thames and sets off in pursuit of Cigar Girl's Sunseeker, racing past Parliament, slicing past wharves, skimming back streets, crashing through a fish market, ploughing into a restaurant and executing a perfect 360 degree barrel roll before hurtling into the topical shadow of the Millennium Dome. Brosnan even finds time to slyly adjust his tie. Underwater. For a British audience there's a palpably patriotic rush in seeing Bond bring widescreen action beats to home shores. It feels like a victory lap for the dying days of Cool Britannia.

"RENARD'S BEHIND THIS"

For all that SPECTRE declared the cause of terror in their acronym, Renard is the first true terrorist villain that Bond has faced. It's a choice of foe that nods to the real world's infamous Carlos the Jackal, finally captured in 1997 and so absorbed by pop culture that his face adorns the cover of Black Grape's It's Great When You're Straight... Yeah.

Renard is sold to us as an anarchist – "His only goal is chaos" – and, in a neat but ultimately wasted touch, a bullet worming through his medulla oblonga has annihilated his senses, leaving him impervious to pain. "You cannot kill me," he states, ashen and almost vampiric. "I am already dead."

Equally intriguingly, he's clearly maddened by Elektra's talk of Bond being a good lover (sexual jealousy is an untapped but potent motivation for any aspiring maniac confronted by 007). As Renard, Robert Carlyle brings the residual heat of his recent starmaking turns in *Trainspotting* and *The Full Monty* but he struggles to summon the baleful charisma the role demands. Yes, there's the faintest ghost of Donald Pleasence's Blofeld in his scar-cracked face, but too often "the world's greatest terrorist" resembles nothing so much as a disenfranchised nightclub bouncer.

THE VULNERABLE BOND

There's a hole blown in the side of MI6 HQ and it feels like an impossible wound at the very heart of our hero's world.

We've witnessed 007 experiencing moments of vulnerability before, of course – cradling his slain bride in *On Her Majesty's Secret Service* or stumbling, half-broken, from the centrifuge in *Moonraker* – but *The World Is Not Enough* goes out of its way to bruise and humanise Bond. He caps the traditionally triumphant pre-titles by smashing into the Millennium Dome, then plummets, clinging to dear life before his injured silhouette limps into the opening credits. When we next see him he's nursing a bandaged arm and attending a sombre Scottish funeral. It's as if the Kryptonite of consequences has finally infiltrated this suave superman's life.

Bond's vulnerability isn't just physical in this movie – his licence to kill clearly takes a cut of his soul, too. The ultimate consequence of his calling comes when he despatches Elektra, just as she teases him with the words "James! You can't kill me! Not in cold blood!" But he does, because he needs to, and because he won't allow it to touch him. It's the closest the big screen Bond has come to that stark, numbed line in Fleming's *Casino Royale*: "The bitch is dead now." No wonder the screenwriters toyed with using it.

INTERCEPTED INTELLIGENCE:

As Fleming tells us in On Her Majesty's Secret Service, "The World Is Not Enough" is Bond's ancestral motto.

Peter Jackson and Joe Dante were early contenders to direct this film.

It took six weeks to shoot the Thames boat chase sequence – and endless permissions. The Counter-terrorist Unit was particularly interested in the nature of the explosions around the Dome.

Long-forgotten topical gag: one of the wheel-clampers soaked by Bond's boat is Ray Brown, briefly notorious star of reality TV show *The Clampers*.

Christmas Jones's look recalls PlayStation icon Lara Croft, then at the height of her popularity.

The legendary Scott Walker recorded an end credits song, but it was ultimately dropped.

DIE ANOTHER DAY

2002 133 minutes

Director: Lee Tamahori

Writers: Neal Purvis, Robert Wade

Score: David Arnold

Title song: Madonna

Cast: Pierce Brosnan, Halle Barry, Toby Stephens, Rosamund Pike, John Cleese

SEX FOR DINNER, DEATH FOR BREAKFAST

Propelled by a breathless cartoon energy, *Die Another Day* wants to weld the alternating currents of the Bond franchise – grounded spycraft and reality-orbiting fantasy.

It plays like some disorientating double bill of *From Russia With Love* and *Moonraker*. The first half courts an authentic Fleming flavour, dealing with the repercussions of Bond's imprisonment by the North Koreans and placing our hero in an intrigue-soaked Cuba, a backdrop that feels like a lost corner of the early '60s where the Cold War remains within touching distance.

And then the movie lurches into romp mode, summoning the plausibility-baiting spirit of Bond's '70s incarnation. It's astonishing just how far this film pushes the SF elements outlawed by *For Your Eyes Only*: invisible car aside, we also have gene therapy machines with the power to trade races, an armoured exo-skeleton torn from the pages of Marvel Comics and a virtual reality device on a technological par with *Star Trek: The Next Generation*'s 24th Century holodeck.

Ironically, helmer Lee Tamahori was best known for *Once Were Warriors*, a bare-knuckled drama dealing with issues of immigration in his native New Zealand. "I was concerned that Bond had lost a little of its thriller edge," he declared, while delivering an entry that loosened the bolts of reality for the first time in two decades.

SURF'S UP!

At first there's an ominous thrum of water, the sound of a colossal wave with clear designs on the North Korean coast. And then three figures on surfboards emerge, keeping tight formation as they ride this towering surge of ocean.

American surf king Laird Hamilton oversaw this spectacular opening sequence, finding a starring role for a fabled Hawaiian wave named – appropriately – Jaws. It's a

169

humbling piece of showmanship that launches the twentieth Bond film in fine style, true to the franchise's tradition of flesh-scraping, bone-risking stuntcraft. But elsewhere *Die Another Day* also sees this tradition sacrificed to Hollywood's creeping reliance on CGI. An infamous scene finds a digital 007 parasailing between weightless glaciers, surfing a PlayStation sea. As phoney as a chocolate Oddjob, it feels like a betrayal of something fundamental to the Bond ethos.

SIGMUND FREUD, ANALYSE THIS

For once the title sequence isn't the usual self-contained glamour show. We've already seen movie narrative bleed into the main titles – a wounded Bond limps into the opening credits of *The World Is Not Enough* while *GoldenEye* recaps the collapse of communism via the educational medium of supermodels. *Die Another Day* takes this still further, transforming Danny Kleinman's titles into a crucial chain-link in the film's storyline.

Captured by the North Koreans, Bond is subjected to 14 months of torture, a passage of time that's sold to us in a parade of hallucinatory images. Women form from ice, half angels of comfort, half figures of threat. Glistening, oil-black scorpions swarm across the screen. Molten succubi taunt our hero. Is this a glimpse into Bond's fracturing mind as he fights to keep his psyche intact? Is every Bond title sequence simply a Freudian rummage in 007's unconscious? Isn't Madonna's clattering title song torture enough?

A CAR TOO FAR?

"We call it the Vanish," puns Q, irresistibly, revealing Bond's latest – and most contentious – set of wheels. The introduction of the Aston Martin V12 Vanquish marks the return of the franchise's time-honoured marque, restored to centre stage now that a three-film deal with BMW has expired. Naturally it bristles with armaments, from missiles to machine-guns, and even finds a place for the design-classic ejector seat in its arsenal of gizmology.

More problematically, it's also capable of turning invisible. As John Cleese's cranky MI6 gadget-head explains, the car uses experimental adaptive camouflage tech: tiny cameras on one side project the image they see onto a light-emitting polymer skin on the other, creating a kind of reality-jamming cloaking device. Production designer Peter Lamont insisted this was perfectly credible – he even claimed to have obtained a government white paper on the subject – but for many this was a slice of spy-fi too far. You can only imagine the incredulous ghost of Connery.

JINXING IT

Halle Berry rises from the blue, sun-pounded shimmer of the Mediterrean, an A-list Venus in a tangerine bikini, a blade on her hip. It's a direct homage to Ursula Andress's immortal entrance in *Dr. No*, of course, but while this visual ensured a place for *Die Another Day* in the pages of the world's tabloids, the film's female lead was looking to higher things. The day Berry shot Jinx's screen-melting debut was the day she discovered her nomination for the Oscar she'd ultimately win for *Monster's Ball*. All that Academy-swaying talent can't quite save her from fumbling the franchise's trademark one-liners: "Oh yeah, I think I got the... thrust... of it," she smirks, the words crashing like lumps of raw, unprocessed innuendo from her lips.

HAPPY ANNIVERSARY, MISTER BOND

Nostalgia is an unsung emotion in Bond's universe. And small wonder, given the unsentimental, battle-calloused nature of its hero.

We've seen the occasional callback to previous adventures – Lazenby's regretful rooting through Connery's desk in *On Her Majesty's Secret Service*, the mischievously throwaway resurrection of Blofeld in *For Your Eyes Only* – but the films traditionally shun the kind of fan-pleasing continuity touches found in other franchises.

Die Another Day is different. Celebrating the twin milestones of forty years and twenty movies, it plays like a wink-loaded stock-take of Bond history. Q's lab in particular is a veritable Christie's auction house of iconic props, from Rosa Klebb's poison-spiked shoe to *Octopussy*'s stealth-gator to *Thunderball*'s mini-breather and jetpack ("Does this still work?" twinkles Brosnan, with just a hint of fanboy glee).

Tamahori also quotes some of the franchise's most treasured visuals, from *Spy*'s Union Jack parachute to Honey Ryder's bikini-powered introduction in *Dr. No*. Elsewhere there's the futurist echo of Ken Adam's Atlantis in the crystalline contours of Graves's ice palace.

Crushed with kisses to the past, *Die Another Day* is the first truly self-regarding Bond film, a valentine to its own legend. Yes, it's a birthday bash – but it's also perilously close to a heritage park, a franchise in danger of choking on its own mythology (Madonna's cry of "I'm going to avoid the cliché" in the theme song suddenly feels like a lone subversive voice). Even the title is a focus group away from some self-parodying horror like *You Never Die Once*.

Perhaps, the filmmakers came to suspect, it was finally time to smash the Bond brand – and rebuild it.

INTERCEPTED INTELLIGENCE

Bond examines a copy of Field Guide To Birds Of The West Indies, the book whose author's "brief, unromantic and yet very masculine" name Fleming stole for his hero.

The flight attendant on Bond's return to Britain is played by Roger Moore's daughter Deborah.

A shot of a vintage Player's Cigarettes poster nods to a line in Fleming's original novel of Thunderball – Domino had a crush on the sailor in the painting.

The film had no title when it was introduced to the world's media at a January 2002 press conference. The press pack simply referred to it as *Bond 20*.

MGM considered a solo franchise for Jinx.

Miranda Frost was originally written as Gala Brand, Fleming's heroine in Moonraker.

London Calling by The Clash is the first time a genuine pop song has been used on a Bond soundtrack (*A View To A Kill*'s California Girls was a soundalike version).

CASINO ROYALE

2006 144 minutes

Director: Martin Campbell

Writers: Neal Purvis, Robert Wade, Paul Haggis

Score: David Arnold

Title song: Chris Cornell

Cast: Daniel Craig, Eva Green, Mads Mikkelsen, Giancarlo Giannini, Jeffrey Wright

THE COLDEST BLOOD

He steps towards us through a storm of playing cards, a faceless, ink-dark silhouette transformed into flesh and blood. He has a boxer's countenance, quite at odds with his faultlessly tailored suit. His eyes are a frightening, vengeful blue, like glaciers on fire. "The coldest blood runs through my veins," declares the testosterone surge of the title song, and in that moment you feel the chill of this man. Meet the new James Bond: reborn, rebuilt, rebooted.

Released in 2006, a long four years on from *Die Another Day*, *Casino Royale* proves a muscular reinvention of the Bond brand, one that obliterates four decades of big screen mythology. The filmmakers had contemplated the prequel

175

option before – as we've established, 1987's *The Living Daylights* was set to focus on a neophyte 007, winning his licence to kill. Cubby Broccoli dismissed the idea, convinced audiences would never buy the notion of a rookie Bond. But now the prequel was prime Hollywood currency, reinvigorating rival franchises from *Batman* to *Star Wars*. In a sense Bond was once again chasing big screen fashion, just as *Moonraker* had so opportunistically scrambled after the space fantasy dollar.

But deeper creative impulses were at play. While *Die Another Day* had proved Pierce Brosnan's most triumphant mission at the box office, the producers were determined to arrest the franchise's slide into the fantastical. The true life horror of 9/11 also shaped their desire to forge a new Bond, one conceived as a tactical response to a fundamentally more terrifying world.

They returned to the wellspring of Ian Fleming. Published in 1953, Casino Royale was the first Bond novel, the darkly elegant big bang of all that was to follow. It was a choice that Brosnan championed – he had even conspired with Quentin Tarantino on a pitch for an authentic period adaptation – but the fifth James Bond found himself unceremoniously dismissed from Her Majesty's secret service ("It was disappointing, it was surprising and I accepted the knowledge after 24 hours of being in shock," he shared, clearly wounded). "I will replace you", vows *Casino Royale*'s brash title song, and for once the traditional gentlemanly transition between Bonds feels like a death match. Guess who wins?

THUG CULTURE

"He's someone you don't want to have an argument with at the bar," said director Martin Campbell of his bruising new star. For all that Daniel Craig takes a blowtorch to the cinematic myth of Bond as some suave, unflappable charm-bomb, his brute-in-a-suit chimes with Fleming's original conception of the character: in You Only Live Twice Blofeld dismisses the fastidious, worldly 007 as "a common thug, a blunt instrument wielded by dolts in high places."

More pugilist than playboy, Craig's Bond takes inspiration from the actor's time on *Munich*, the 2005 thriller whose set he shared with technical advisors from Mossad and the British secret service: "You can see it in their eyes. You know immediately – oh, hello, he's a killer. There's a look. These guys walk into a room and very subtly they check the perimeters for an exit. That's the sort of thing I wanted." Roger Moore, you imagine, might subtly check the vintage of the Chateau Mouton Rothschild instead.

Defined by his compelling blue-ice gaze, Craig's teutonic, distinctly weatherworn looks delivered a radical new face for Bond, earning him a firestorm of abuse from the more vicious and judgmental corners of the press and the internet. Incensed, he fed his ire into his performance, igniting the kerosene smoulder that would come to define his Bond: "It did spur me," he revealed. "I did think 'It was going to be good before. Now it's really going to be good.'"

Craig's musclebound, butcher's window torso lets the film deliver another profound reinvention of the Bond myth. Homaging Ursula Andress's timeless entrance in *Dr. No*, he rises from the sea in a pair of equally immortal blue speedos, a moment that explicitly sexualises 007 himself for the first time in the franchise's history. It feels like long belated payback. Somewhere, you suspect, Honey Ryder watches from beneath a mango tree and smiles.

LICENCE TO KILL

The opening moments of *Casino Royale* form an instant mission statement. Tellingly - disorientatingly - the customary gunbarrel sequence is stolen from us. No parade of blank white circles punctures the anticipatory dark of the cinema, no familiar Monty Norman overture hurries our pulses. Bond, we realise, must earn these iconic trappings, just as he earns his licence to kill with the two contrasting kills we will shortly witness.

The opening shot places us in the frost and the steam of the Prague night, an eternal heartland of espionage whose lingering Cold War ghosts are captured in crisp monochrome. Bond waits in a darkened room, an assassin in the shadows, just like his fateful rendezvous with Dent in *Dr. No*. This kill is smooth, functional, sardonic. It's intercut with an altogether uglier encounter. In flashback a snarling Bond brawls with a man in a toilet, a brutal scrap presented to us in grainy footage reminiscent of a surveillance cam, slamming into the classy noir stylings of the main narrative. It's raw, vicious, intense and, above all, messy, the kind of bloody kill that stains Bond's hands, his suit and his soul. Yes, he wins his licence to kill for us, with all the thrill-loaded promise that entails. But maybe, just for a moment, we feel less an audience and more like accessories to murder.

KEEP ON RUNNING

Bond's remorseless pursuit of scarred bomb-maker Mollaka is one of the most satisfying action sequences yet – a defiantly physical reproach to the audience-swindling CGI of *Die Another Day*. He's clumsy but winningly gutsy in the chase, clearly lacking the free-running expertise of his quarry but compensating with balls, determination and ingenuity (when he's not commandeering a bulldozer the inexorable agent is smashing through a plaster wall with just the faintest touch of Wile E Coyote about him). Framed against clear Madagascan skies, the confrontation on the towering cranes of a construction site has a vertiginous sense of reality – and when Bond effortlessly catches the gun that a desperate Mollaka lobs at him it's a moment of masterful, minimalist cool. This exhaustively choreographed sequence took six weeks to shoot, with real life free-running specialist Sebastien Foucan cast as the fleet-heeled terrorist.

"I'VE GOT A LITTLE ITCH…"

"It's the simplest thing to cause you more pain than you can endure…"

007's torture by Le Chiffre may be the moment the franchise finally separates from its cosy fixture as a Christmas Day TV mainstay. Bloodied, bound, stripped naked, Bond is repeatedly thrashed around the groin by a coiled hank of rope. There's a faddish hint of *Hostel*-style horror in the grime and meat hooks of the staging but this scene is present in all its leg-crossing glory in Fleming's original novel – though the literary Le Chiffre favours a carpet beater rather than a length of rope.

The studio was troubled by its inclusion in the screenplay but the filmmakers were determined not to compromise on its essential ferocity (the stuntman doubling

Daniel Craig was more troubled by the thought of performing nude, a prospect he found petrifying). Our hero's initial animal howls are genuinely distressing, but within moments the scene tilts into delicious black comedy. "I've got a little itch…" gasps Bond, somehow, impossibly, finding the upper hand in this bleakest of situations. "Would you mind? No, no, no… to the right! To the right!" It's a pivotal moment for the screen Bond. He's just discovered that gallows humour is the best defence against the ever-circling promise of death. Every dark one liner to come is born here.

"HALF-MONK, HALF-HITMAN"

Casino Royale takes the raw matter of James Bond – one of MI6's "maladjusted young men", taunts Vesper Lynd – and builds a screen icon around him. But there's a cost involved. "You do what I do for too long and there won't be any soul left to salvage," he tells Vesper, and we soon learn the truth of this.

Bond slays a machete-wielding assailant and, in the aftermath of the kill, strips himself to the waist, scrubs away the blood, swills neat alchohol and confronts himself in the mirror, his gaze urgent, searching, clearly wondering what's become of his humanity. And then he holds a shell-shocked Vesper in the shower, suddenly tender, protective, still human. Her death removes even this sliver of salvation.

The final scene finds him stepping into shot like some Savile Row Terminator, his suit immaculate, his outsized gun an unmistakable Freudian statement. The signature theme finally begins to prowl after being denied to us for too long. "The name's Bond," he declares, "James Bond." It feels like a triumph for the icon, a tragedy for the man.

THIS NEVER HAPPENED TO THE OTHER FELLAS

So just how many James Bonds make six? For all that this reboot sets out to scorch the past, *Casino Royale* proves the most persuasive argument yet for one of the wilder theories in Bond fandom – James Bond is simply a codename, a title to be earned, a nom de espionnage bestowed upon the best and deadliest operative on the MI6 payroll.

Yes, *Casino* wants to be a clean slate, but even director Martin Campbell admitted "If you think about the timeline, it makes no sense". Judi Dench's M is a clear holdover from the Brosnan era, after all (unless she's playing some subtly different alternate reality version of the secret service matriarch).

The idea of the government wielding Bond as some indestructible concept rather than a single mortal man has a certain appeal. If it's true, it's small wonder diabolical masterminds shudder when he announces his name – he may as well suavely declare "I'm warfare... Bio-chemical warfare!". And, if you squint, the theory makes a kind of sense when applied to the history of the franchise.

Perhaps Lazenby's young, sensitive Bond was broken by the death of his wife, leading to the recall of Connery, whose despatch of Blofeld in *Diamonds Are Forever* always feels more a callous piece of business than the culmination of some fiery vendetta. You can easily imagine Roger Moore's surprisingly long-lived incarnation finally retiring to charm the blue-blooded beauties of Monaco. And perhaps Dalton's Bond got a taste for the life of a freelance "problem eliminator" after going rogue in *Licence To Kill*.

There are glitches in this theory, of course. Brosnan's introduction in *GoldenEye* takes place in 1986, exactly midway between Moore and Dalton in the true-life timeline (though a nice nod to the fact that Brosnan so nearly won the role that year). And why would each new Bond acknowledge the death of Tracy, even to the extent of placing flowers on her grave? Perhaps she's an eternal symbol of everything they must sacrifice to be this man.

Die Another Day helmer Lee Tamahori fought to bring the multiple Bonds theory to the screen – "You either believe that it's the same guy all along, and he just keeps being played by different actors, or you ascribe to the view that I have which is that Connery and all the others were actually different guys with the 007 prefix" – but he was overruled.

How many James Bonds make six? Ultimately, there's only one answer. There are six James Bonds. And only one Bond... James Bond.

INTERCEPTED INTELLIGENCE

Casino Royale was brought to the screen as a TV adaptation in 1954 and a big screen spoof in 1967. Eon reclaimed the rights in 1999.

Shortlisted Bonds included *ER*'s Goran Visnjic, Sam Worthington and a 22 year old Henry Cavill.

Martin Campbell took direct inspiration from *The Ipcress File* for the film's moody, espionage-drenched opening scene.

While a proposed solo film for *Die Another Day*'s Jinx was eventually abandoned, the script's more personal, grounded take on the character inspired the screenwriters' approach to *Casino Royale*.

Vesper's scarlet dress in the Venice scenes is a direct homage to Nic Roeg's *Don't Look Now*.

Danny Kleinman's title sequence took inspiration from the cover of the first edition of Casino Royale.

Look for cameos by two past Bond girls: *Thunderball*'s Diane Hartwood and *You Only Live Twice*'s Tsai Chin.

QUANTUM OF SOLACE

2008 106 minutes

Director: Marc Forster

Writers: Paul Haggis, Neal Purves, Robert Wade

Score: David Arnold

Title song: Jack White and Alicia Keyes

Cast: Daniel Craig, Olga Kurylenko, Mathieu Almaric, Gemma Arterton, Giancarlo Giannini

QUANTUM THEORY

While it's a welcome touch of genuine Fleming in a film whose theme song inflicts the lyric "Another blinger with a slick trigger finger for Her Majesty", *Quantum Of Solace* may be the most confounding title in the franchise's history.

The best Bond titles evoke a certain scorpion-on-a-tombstone shiver (*You Only Live Twice*, *Live And Let Die*) or find a menacing poetry in the name of their antagonist (*Dr. No*, *Goldfinger*). The worst fall into dead-eyed pastiche (*Licence To Kill*, *Die Another Day*). *Quantum Of Solace* is in a class of its own – oblique, inscrutable, just on the edge of pretentious, it's a marvel it made it through the focus groups.

186

Fleming clearly relished the phrase; he slipped it into Thrilling Cities, his anthology of true life travel writing, but it's best known as the name of a short story in For Your Eyes Only, 1960's collection of bite-sized Bond tales. This slight, Somerset Maugham-indebted morality piece was as much a departure for Fleming as the first-person crime romance of The Spy Who Loved Me. Essentially a marital anecdote related to Bond at a dinner party, it's no surprise that all that made it to the screen were the three unfathomable words that christened it.

"I was unsure at first," confessed Daniel Craig, clearly as perplexed as anyone as he prepared for his encore mission as 007. "Bond is looking for his quantum of solace and that's what he wants. He wants his closure." The film's name was only locked days before the press launch in January 2008. Given the symbolic import of Vesper's Algerian loveknot necklace it's a wonder the Bondmakers didn't plump for another unclaimed Fleming title: The Property Of A Lady.

CRACKING THE CODA

There's only ever been the thinnest connective tissue between Bond films. *From Russia With Love* finds 007 picnicking with Sylvia Trench, an old flame from *Dr. No*, while the ruthless quest for Blofeld that launches *Diamonds Are Forever* can be read as the act of a vengeful widower chasing closure after the tragic climax of *On Her Majesty's Secret Service*. For the most part, however, they exist as hermetically sealed missions.

Quantum Of Solace is the anomaly: conceived as a direct continuation of *Casino Royale*, it's the first sequel in the Bond canon. The opening sequence follows the closing moments of *Casino*, a freshly knee-capped Mr White stashed in the back of Bond's Aston and his cronies in road-scorching pursuit.

For Bond the death of Vesper is an open wound, and it brings us a hero even more implacable than the burning-eyed avenger of *Licence To Kill*. "This man and I have unfinished business," he states, with a quiet chill, as he finally confronts her treacherous boyfriend. For the first time the demons that 007 faces are inner ones, impervious to marksmanship and quips. In truth, *Quantum Of Solace* feels more a coda to *Casino Royale* than a genuine sequel, one last bullet rather than a fresh round.

THE BOURNE LEGACY

An ominous rumble and roar of cars as the camera races over water. A blink of silver bodywork. Tight flash of cold, cobalt eyes. And then a slam of accelerator. Gunfire, speed, peril.

Welcome to the opening moments of *Quantum Of Solace*, a car chase cut so brutally you almost expect the celluloid to bleed.

It's an audacious statement of intent by director Marc Forster, sacrificing any sense of the spatial for a breathless sensory assault. For Forster it was all about the instant: the tyranny of the moment rather than the broader spectacle. He wanted *Quantum* to be "tight and fast... like a bullet", and his use of frantic flash-cuts and fast-blurring, hand-held camerawork finds 007 in thrall to the Jason Bourne movies (they even poached second unit director Dan Bradley, who worked on 2004's *The Bourne Supremacy* and 2007's *The Bourne Ultimatum*).

It proved a divisive artistic choice. Even former members of Her Majesty's Secret Service weighed in. "It was just like a commercial of the action," judged ex-Bond Roger Moore. "There didn't seem to be any geography and you were wondering what the hell was going on."

"YOU DON'T EVEN KNOW WE EXIST"

"The first thing you should know about us is that we have people everywhere," declares Mr White. It's our earliest inkling of the terrifying shadow-power of Quantum, the first international cartel that Bond has faced since the days of SPECTRE.

As globe-menacing syndicates go, it's a very different proposition to Blofeld and his boiler-suited boys. Composed of plutocrats and nation-shapers, the famous and the faceless, the people who step behind the doors of the world, Quantum nods to such true life phenomena as the Bilderberg Group and all the conspiracy theories that cling to it. You imagine their after-hours jollies include the kind of whisperingly exclusive Venetian-masked orgies Tom Cruise stumbles upon in *Eyes Wide Shut*. Quantum's intriguingly apolitical – "We deal with the left or the right, with dictators or liberators" – and in many ways is more a lethal, wormy meme than a physical threat.

A NIGHT AT THE OPERA

Bond confronts the murmuring might of Quantum at the lakeside opera house in Bregenz, Austria. This floating stage, dominated by a vast, Daliesque eyeball, makes for a stunning backdrop to what's the most unequivocally arty moment in Bond history. As Tosca begins to soar, 007's gaze locks with the psychotic glare of Dominic Greene. The moment holds, finally broken by silent flashes of gunfire. The opera surges. Bond races through a burning kitchen, the flames and bullet-play intercut with the make-believe bloodshed onstage. All the while that giant eye watches, its iris contracting like the gaze of some disdainful god. It's a unique, bravura sequence, arthouse cinema as mainstream thrills.

LOCATION LOCATION

For all that its reputation is coloured by the whip-smash chaos of its action sequences, *Quantum Of Solace* also remembers to breathe. And, when it does, Mark Forster delivers a film that's surprisingly elegant - and impeccably well travelled.

Shot in no less than six countries, it enjoyed more time on location than any other Bond adventure. A cosmopolitan Swiss/German, Forster ached to flee the studio-bound kingdoms of Pinewood, keen for his film to absorb the atmospheres of real places. He proves to have a fine eye for local colour, and there's something of the anthropologist about him, too. For once Bond locations aren't the usual Cinzano billboard fantasies. These environments feel real, lived in, alive with the texture of native culture. The shanty towns of Haiti are brought to the screen with a vibrant sense of decay while Forster takes pains to show us the people of Bolivia, the very ones threatened by the amoral machinations of Quantum.

From Talamare to the Atacama Desert, Port Au Prince to La Paz, Lake Garda to Lake Constance, *Quantum Of Solace* is the gentleman traveller of the Bond franchise. You imagine even Ian Fleming might approve – when not tutting down his cigarette holder at the confounded racket of the title song.

INTERCEPTED INTELLIGENCE

Originally there were three Alfa Romeos chasing Bond in the pre-titles. Forster felt the sequence was overlong so brutally recut it to show only two.

The car chase was filmed with the Ultimate Arm, a five-axis, gyro-stabilised crane camera mounted on top of a high-speed vehicle.

Daniel Craig sliced off the tip of his fingertip during a fight sequence.

Mathieu Almaric wanted to wear prosthetics for his role as Dominic Greene but Marc Forster dissuaded him, keen to emphasise the "hidden evil" of Quantum rather than anything tangibly monstrous.

Agent Fields' first name is Strawberry, but it's never uttered onscreen. That gag is reserved for the credits.

Guillermo del Toro – a friend of Forster's – provides various voices in the film.

The climax was originally set in the Swiss Alps but Forster switched it to the desert, wanting the major action sequences to echo the four elements of earth, water, air and fire.

SKYFALL

2012 143 minutes

Director: Sam Mendes

Writers: Neal Purvis, Robert Wade, John Logan

Score: Thomas Newman

Title song: Adele

Cast: Daniel Craig, Judi Dench, Javier Bardem, Bérénice Lim Marlohe, Ralph Fiennes

BULLDOG SPIRIT

Marking half a century of James Bond on the big screen, *Skyfall* was a juggernaut, the first of the franchise to haul over a billion dollars at the box office.

But it wasn't just riding a groundswell of nostalgia, weaponising 50 years of audience affection. There were other cultural tides at work. That summer saw Her Majesty's secret servant recruited for security detail at the London Olympics – with Her Majesty herself on comic relief duty alongside a deadpan Daniel Craig in a skit directed by Danny Boyle. There was a patriotic surge in Britain in 2012 and a little of that red, white and blue buzz attached itself to the golden anniversary

Bond film, an entry that not only celebrated Britain's premier cinematic hero but made London and the Scottish Highlands core parts of its storytelling landscape.

Helmed by Oscar-winning Sam Mendes, acclaimed for his work on both the stage and the screen, *Skyfall* is also the first Heritage Bond: handsomely shot and emotionally grounded, it feels like a high-end, hand-tooled luxury product, pulp fiction with a designer label. There's a whiff of walnut-trim and fresh leather about it. And just as *Quantum of Solace* chased Bourne so this movie is in thrall to Christopher Nolan's steely, psychologically complex Batman movies, especially 2008's *The Dark Knight*, from which it cribs some hero/villain dynamics.

"Nolan proved that you can make a huge movie that is thrilling and entertaining and has a lot to say about the world we live in," said Mendes, freely admitting his inspiration as he transitioned from arthouse to blockbuster mode. "That did help give me the confidence to take this movie in directions that, without *The Dark Knight*, might not have been possible."

"OLD DOG, NEW TRICKS"

It may be the golden anniversary Bond movie but *Skyfall* isn't afraid to upend tradition. This much is obvious from a pre-titles sequence that climaxes with a bullet-torn 007 plummeting from a train. Unlike the showstopping plunges that launched *The Spy Who Loved Me*, *Moonraker* and *GoldenEye*, this isn't played as a triumphant moment of spectacle, something for an audience to applaud. Bond seems tiny, almost doll-like, as he falls, a man surrendering to destiny. It's the year of the London Olympics but there's no Union Jack parachute to save the day, just the first doomy chords of Adele's theme song as he smashes into the water.

Elsewhere the film is equally keen to shake up the tropes. Ben Whishaw's new Q brings a snotty hipster attitude to the cherished gadgetry of yesterday ("You were expecting an exploding pen?"). The final showdown is all shotguns and nail-bombs, a scrappy, makeshift battle that's closer to the home-brewed violence of *Straw Dogs* than the classic lair-under-siege skirmishes of *You Only Live Twice* or *Spy*. And, with M's death occurring on his watch, Bond essentially fails. *Skyfall* masquerades as a fiftieth anniversary celebration. Beneath the nostalgia it's just as much a radical inversion of a winning formula.

THE PRICE OF SILVA

All bleached hair and Eurotrash swagger, Javier Bardem returns a sense of theatricality to the Bond villain. His performance as cyber-terrorist supreme Raoul Silva is very much an old school turn, full of delight at his own louche menace. "Hello, James," he purrs, entering the movie as if it belongs to him. "Do you like the island?"

Silva's presented to us as 007's shadow, a brilliant ex-MI6 agent who now chooses his own missions, free from obligation to Queen and country. It's a familiar figure; from Red Grant to Scaramanga to Alec Trevelyan we've seen so many of these dark reflections across the years. What makes Silva the perfect ironic counterpoint for this golden anniversary is that, for all his glorious exploits, all those adventures, he's Bond without the franchise. He has no fans, no legacy, no box-sets, no brand. Even the object of his obsession denies him the right to rival 007. "I barely remember you at all," says M, an admission that must burn like the hydrogen cyanide that ravaged his face (the moment Silva removes his dental plate he's revealed as a ghoulish hybrid of mastermind and henchman, part-Zorin, part-Jaws, the ultimate chimera of a Bond bad guy). Soon, he's told, his past will be as non-existent as his future.

Bond and Silva may be "the last two rats" but in the end there's room for only one stylish, charismatic superspy on this screen.

SKYFALL IS WHERE WE START

"From an actor's point of view, Bond presented terrible problems," Sean Connery once lamented. "He has no mother. He has no father. He doesn't come from anywhere. He hasn't been anywhere before he became 007. He was born 33 years old."

Skyfall takes many cues from Christopher Nolan's Batman movies but its most blatant echo is giving Bond a secret origin story. While Ian Fleming established that Bond lost his parents in a climbing accident – fleetingly referenced in *GoldenEye* – Sam Mendes makes it the kind of textbook orphan-spawning tragedy that creates superheroes. We even see the graves, a gothic note that recalls all those comic book panels of a young Bruce Wayne, vowing vengeance by the headstones of his slain parents.

Bond's Scottish background was a biographical wrinkle Fleming only added in You Only Live Twice, a sly way to justify Connery's accent on the big screen, but here the geography defines the man. The brute, sunless beauty of the Highlands is the landscape that forged Bond, all burly peaks and mists that cling like secrets. Skyfall Lodge itself is a clear counterpart to Wayne Manor, complete with hidden tunnels that parallel the subterranean womb of the Batcave, which swallowed Bruce as a child. Batman kept his ancestral seat but for Bond this is an exorcism as much as a homecoming. There's a mythic resonance to this abandoned, memory-scarred place, even though it's a wholly new addition to the lore.

BETWEEN TWO WORLDS

Ravishingly photographed by Roger Deakins – who had collaborated with Sam Mendes on *Jarhead* and *Revolutionary Road* – *Skyfall* places Bond in two distinct worlds. Two distinct realities, almost.

Deakins paints the East as a shimmering fever dream: Shanghai is a neon fantasia, a city of illumination and shadow, the landscape of espionage itself. In one especially ornamental setpiece Bond fights in silhouette against a wall of pulsing electric light and for once the audience is encouraged to admire the art as well as taste the adrenaline. Macau, too, feels a little unreal, an opulent, decadent backdrop where Komodo dragons prowl casinos and smoky-eyed femme fatales await their man. Bond, we know, belongs in this world.

But *Skyfall*, the most patriotic of these big screen capers, also insists that Bond belongs in Britain. Gloomy, autumnal, contemporary Britain, all blues and greys, concrete and drizzle. "Welcome to rush hour on the Tube," teases Q. "Not something you'd know much about." And it's certainly a jolt to see 007 brushing shoulders with everyday Londoners, in all their *Antiques Roadshow* bystander glory. This is the unseen, unsung Britain he's fighting for. The same one he's always fought for, even if he's never truly seemed part of it before.

THE QUEEN IS DEAD

Sam Mendes had a death wish and Judi Dench's indomitable Queen of Numbers was in his sights. "You can't kill him; let's kill her instead!" he remembered thinking. "I thought I was going to get so much shit for that. But you know how you shock people into rediscovering their first acquaintance with the characters…"

The final act of *Skyfall* not only casts M as de facto Bond girl, riding in the passenger seat of the Aston Martin, it also makes her the equally traditional sacrificial lamb, a role fulfilled by everyone from *Goldfinger*'s Jill Masterson to Agent Fields in *Quantum of Solace*. Usually such deaths are plot pivots, mid-movie jolts. Here it's an ending. Of course its not the most tragic climax to a Bond movie – Tracy's murder in *On Her Majesty's Secret Service* still hits harder, for all that Dench, after seven films, is a more established screen presence – but it's the first time the MI6 family has taken a direct hit. Usually M, Q and Moneypenny are quietly recast as the franchise shuffles faces between films. This time there's blood, and something fundamentally changes in the Bond universe.

The cosy, unspoken pact between audience and filmmakers that keeps beloved characters safe is irrevocably broken.

"THE INEVITABILITY OF TIME"

Our first glimpse of Bond is a spindly, nebulous silhouette, approaching the camera like some *Close Encounters* alien emerging from the mothership. But while the traditional gunbarrel intro is still denied us this isn't the half-formed 007 of *Casino Royale* and *Quantum*, the raw recruit that rebooted and reblooded the franchise.

Skyfall accelerates Bond's arc, skipping a million unseen missions to present him as a weary veteran. Espionage, he's informed, is "a young man's game". And Craig, in a pinched grey suit that barely contains him, his hair cropped like a Sandhurst cadet, cuts an older, considerably more grizzled figure. Lying low after taking the bullet in Istanbul he drinks, screws and plays death games with scorpions. Without his duty to the secret service he's a husk of vices, all those primal impulses that Fleming hung a hero on. Back on a mission he's born again, healed by his own iconography – a spruce, tuxedo-clad Craig strikes his favourite GQ pose as Bond arrives at the floating casino in Macau. But the film never lets us forget Bond's years, determined to frame him as a man out of time in a "brave new world". As he collects what appears to be the original *Goldfinger* Aston Martin from his private London garage he seems, impossibly, as old as the franchise itself.

The final moments of *Skyfall* fetishise the touchstones of a classic Bond briefing scene: M's impregnable, leather-lined door, a folder of covert intelligence hitting a desk, Moneypenny reincarnated and ready for banter. The rough-edged 007 of *Casino Royale* is long gone. James Bond has returned, with pleasure. Cue gunbarrel…

INTERCEPTED INTELLIGENCE

An early working title for the 23rd Bond film was *Once Upon A Spy*.

M's F-bomb is the first clearly audible instance of the word in the Bond films.

Sean Connery was considered for the role of Kincade but Mendes thought the casting would be too distracting.

This is the final Bond movie for trumpet player Derek Watkins, who had worked on every film in the series.

The bottle of Macallan Scotch that Silva offers Bond is a 1962 vintage, a nod to the fiftieth anniversary of *Dr. No*.

Silva's monologue about the rats was inspired by a story *American Beauty* cinematographer Conrad Hall once told Sam Mendes.

SPECTRE

2015 148 minutes

Director: Sam Mendes

Writers: John Logan, Neal Purvis, Robert Wade, Jez Butterworth

Score: Thomas Newman

Title song: Sam Smith

Cast: Daniel Craig, Lea Séydoux, Christoph Waltz, Monica Bellucci, Andrew Scott

"THE POWER THEY HAVE"

"James Bond should always fight Blofeld," reckoned screenwriter John Logan in 2011. The courts, however, had long frustrated this simple mythological truth. The legal skirmish over the rights to Ernst Stavro Blofeld and the SPECTRE organisation had kept these core elements of Fleming lore missing in action since 1971's *Diamonds Are Forever*. On 15 November 2013 MGM and Danjaq, LLC, the holding company responsible for all Bond screen rights, announced that they had finally reached an agreement with the estate of the late Kevin McClory, who had partnered with

Broccoli and Saltzman on *Thunderball* and jealously guarded his stake in its concepts ever since.

Returning director Sam Mendes reintroduces SPECTRE in elegantly disquieting style. Bond infiltrates the cabal's midnight meeting at the Palazzo Cardenza, a location that's a statement of power in itself. Prominently placed on the fringes of Rome, it looks more like a national monument than a secret lair (in reality the exteriors were shot at England's Blenheim Palace, ironically also featured in rival 2015 spy flick *Mission: Impossible – Rogue Nation*). The tension of this scene is masterfully assembled from silence, stillness and shadow, exploding into sudden violence as hench-brute Mr Hinx demonstrates the eye-popping realities of career advancement in Blofeld's employ.

Elusive but insidiously influential, SPECTRE feels like a rebranded Quantum. The iconic weight of its name certainly adds an extra percentage of menace, if only to the audience (Bond's never heard of it). And the Special Executive's concerns have a deeply 21st Century shiver: counterfeit pharmaceuticals, Third World exploitation, human trafficking. "We have placed 160,000 migrated females into the leisure sector," one operative declares, a bureaucratic understatement that's infinitely more chilling than any showy plot to ransom the world with nuclear warheads. Even Mr White, it seems, is repulsed by SPECTRE's monetised amorality. "Our game is our game... But this? Women, children..."

THE DAY OF THE DEAD

It's a cavalcade of bones and skulls, garlands, puppets and black lace, a gothic update on the kind of colourful street carnivals that added a splash of travelogue exoticism to *Thunderball* and *Moonraker*. Mexico City is celebrating Día de Muertos as *Spectre* begins and Bond walks among the throng in a skull mask and top hat that cheekily homage Baron Samedi in *Live And Let Die*. At first we have no idea who he is: he's undercover in his own movie.

The film's spectacular opening was a logistical feat that encompassed 1500 extras, 150 make-up artists, 150 hairdressers and no less than 17 cameras to capture it all. Inspired by *Touch Of Evil* and *Goodfellas*, Mendes stages the first fives minutes to give the illusion of a single unbroken shot. In reality it's six shots, invisibly stitched through "blend points". Entering Bond's hotel our eyes are distracted as the camera passes a visually arresting poster on a door. Inside the bedroom another cut is concealed as a wipe within a pan, revealing Bond in his blue suit. Cinematic sleight-of-hand.

Mendes toyed with the idea of mounting the entire pre-titles sequence in this style but soon realised he needed the energy of the editing room for the climactic helicopter sequence. The kind of action vocabulary pioneered by editor Peter Hunt in the '60s simply couldn't be constrained for long.

"THE CURRENCY OF OUR AGE"

Spectre mirrors the reality of espionage in 2015, a global shadow war of digital ghosts and data theft, fought as much on flash drives and mainframes as out in the field. As the first notes of the Bond theme play over the Columbia logo even the lady with the torch looks complicit.

This is the age of WikiLeaks, Julian Assange and Edward Snowden, the battlefield of big data. While Blofeld covets unlimited access to the combined intelligence of nine countries – Nine Eyes is a clear nod to the real world Five Eyes alliance, whose files were leaked by former NSA contractor Snowden in 2013 – MI6 keeps tabs on 007 via smart blood, cutting-edge nano-tech that reduces their star agent to zeroes and ones, flesh and data. "Surveillance is a fact of life," states M, as the studio behind the film discovered to their cost.

On 24 November 2014, a group calling itself the Guardians of Peace staged a cyber-strike against Sony Pictures, demanding the withdrawal of *The Interview*, a comedy based around a plot to assassinate North Korean leader Kim Jong-un. WikiLeaks later disseminated over 30,000 documents obtained through the hack, including an early draft of the *Spectre* screenplay and private email exchanges between executives and filmmakers, arguing for creative changes. For once the inner dialogue of movie production was laid bare. The lady with the torch had surrendered her secrets and a little of that corporate paranoia inevitably haunts the screen here.

A SCAR IS BORN

Two-time Oscar winner Christoph Waltz is the man fronting the reborn SPECTRE. He had won international fame in 2009 for his turn as the satanically genial Colonel Hans Landa in Tarantino's *Inglourious Basterds* and *Spectre* trades on that association to help recreate Bond's definitive screen foe.

Like Landa, this incarnation of Blofeld is silkily poisonous, the perfect dinner guest, a very different proposition to the crack-eyed gnome of Donald Pleasence or Telly Savalas's socially-climbing thug (the fact he has hair positions him a little closer, at least aesthetically, to Charles Gray). All glacial smile and no socks, he has the air of a fastidious, sadistic surgeon, his expertise in high-tech torture revealing him to be psychopathically clinical as much as a clinical psychopath. "There was nobody inside his skull," Blofeld observes of a dead man's eyes. "Most odd." Production designer Dennis Gassner pegged him as "detailed and precise" and used that character note to make the character's surroundings equally cold and clean.

Pre-publicity tried to hide the return of Blofeld behind the smokescreen identity of Franz Oberhauser. No one believed it for a second. The moment a shadowed Waltz appears at the head of the table at the Palazzo Cardenza, his face obscured in homage to Blofeld's initial screen appearances, it's obvious who he is. This still, small figure is the most commanding presence in the room, clearly big enough to inhabit a legendary and much-missed icon.

THE POWER OF 10

Bond's cars have always had an aspirational shimmer but *Spectre*'s Aston Martin DB10 took the notion of exclusivity to the next level. Only ten of them were ever made. It was a concept car, handmade and bespoke, created in-house by the brand's design and engineering teams.

Sleek and seemingly seamless, the DB10's blade-like spokes and shark-face front add a predatory touch to its smooth grey futurism. For Mendes, however, the car represented a vibe as much as a ride. "I wanted what comes with the cars," he said, "mischief, fun and speed." And it certainly restores a little Moore-era smirk to the franchise. *Skyfall* winked at the idea of the ejector seat but never put it into play. Here it propels Daniel

Craig into the sky. He descends like an angel in a Tom Ford suit, tossing a cheery "Good evening!" to a street cleaner as he discards his parachute. A suave, graceful, *fantastical* figure, big screen Bond incarnate, the ultimate evolution of the raw-edged rookie we met in *Casino Royale*.

"A NICE PATTERN DEVELOPED..."

As ever you can sense the Bond franchise chasing the trade winds of the screen in *Spectre*. While its general aesthetic retains the Nolan influence of its predecessor, *Skyfall*, its narrative is in debt to two things: the rise of the Marvel movie and TV's tilt toward long-form storytelling. Ever since *Iron Man* in 2008 Marvel had proved that audiences will embrace an interconnected universe, one that grew in complexity and resonance with every entry. And as the streaming giants rose in the 2010s, everything from *House of Cards* to *Game of Thrones* suggested that viewers enjoyed having their loyalty rewarded over multiple seasons, equally deepening their investment in these worlds.

Aside from a smattering of continuity touches – the presence of Sylvia Trench in *Dr. No* and *From Russia With Love*; the occasional reference to Tracy – the Bond films traditionally existed as discrete entities, more likely to spring a whole new Felix Leiter on you than explicitly connect

210

themselves to some past plot point. This is how Blofeld can fail to recognise Bond in *On Her Majesty's Secret Service* despite a face-to-face meeting in *You Only Live Twice*. Continuity is simply not a priority. The Bond movies are too fluid, too much in forward momentum for that.

No longer. *Spectre* is a dot-to-dot exercise, out to connect the entirety of the Daniel Craig era. Out to map a universe. *Skyfall*'s Silva – previously presented to us as a standalone menace – is here retconned as part of the same organisation behind Le Chiffre and Dominic Greene. Familiar faces, Vesper Lynd among them, haunt the title sequence, decorate the soon-to-be-detonated ruins of MI6 HQ. And Ernst Stavro Blofeld threads it all, an unseen, unsuspected and, if the filmmakers are being honest, *unimagined* presence in the last three films, now revealed as "the author of all [Bond's] pain." Which essentially makes him Ian Fleming, right?

"GOODBYE, JAMES BOND"

Skyfall ended with Bond restored to duty along with the timeless certainties of M, Moneypenny and a mission briefing. *Spectre*'s ending shatters that status quo. Bond throws away his gun, quits the service, shares a smile with lover Madeleine Swann as they drive away from it all in a gleaming DB5 –

albeit with the Bond theme playing, an inescapable reminder that the swagger of the icon is bigger than the man.

The ending is surprising but it's earned. The film repeatedly questions Bond's obligation to his role as death's right hand man. We first see him as a ghoulish, skull-faced figure in Mexico City, an assassin walking among the living dead. In Rome Lucia Sciarra, freshly widowed, believes that Bond's actions have signed her own death warrant, as if there's something lethally contagious about his presence. "Is this really what you want?" asks Madeleine in the dining car of the train. "Living in the shadows? Hunting, being hunted... always alone?" Bond tells her he's not sure he ever had a choice. But the moment he spares Blofeld on Westminster Bridge he makes that choice, and decisively so.

Spectre saves the man as much as it saves the world. It grants Bond a licence to live. For now, at least.

James Bond will return.

INTERCEPTED INTELLIGENCE

John Logan's original screenplay was titled *The Death Collector*, a chapter title from Ian Fleming's You Only Live Twice.

Logan's draft reimagined Blofeld as an African warlord whose real name was Joseph Ki-Embu.

One of the Aston Martin DB10s sold for £2.4 million in 2016. It cannot be driven on the public road.

Franz Oberhauser is the son of Hannes Oberhauser, a character referenced in Fleming's short story Octopussy.

Mexico City had no Día de Muertos parade before Spectre. Inspired by the film, it's now an annual event.

In 1997 Monica Bellucci was a contender for the role of Paris Carver in *Tomorrow Never Dies*.

The painting on the wall in Madeleine's room at the SPECTRE base is Woman With A Fan by Modigliani, the same one being traded in Shanghai in *Skyfall*. It's still missing in real life.

LICENCE TO CHILL – JAMES BOND AND HORROR

Sometimes we take inspiration from the spaces inbetween.

I've always been intrigued by the shadow realm where James Bond ends and the horror genre begins. It's the intersection I wanted to explore in my first novel, The War in the Dark, a book with a mission to splice spy fiction with the occult. Like all shadow realms its borders are in flux, so any maps we make inevitably shift and twist like a spill of mercury. No reconnaisance mission can ever hope to nail down the exact edges of this treacherous territory, so leave your compass behind as we step into the deeper darkness, on Her Majesty's most secret service…

First, some context, because in the beginning the context was crucial. My earliest memories of Ian Fleming's Bond stories were the Pan paperbacks stacked on the tall shelves of my local Forbuoys newsagent. I knew that they were books for grown-ups, which made them all the more enticing as I stared at their covers. And what alluringly cryptic covers they were, photographic still-life compositions with a decidedly macabre edge: You Only Live Twice places a glistening, beetle-black lobster next to an unsheathed samurai knife; Dr No juxtaposes a gun with three white sticks for the blind, their handles curling like skeletal fingers; Thunderball shows a shattered underwater breathing mask, the splintered glass almost like a ruined clockface. Looking at these images now they strike me as borderline ritualistic, like ceremonial items gathered for a dark purpose.

And the company they kept in Forbuoys certainly suggested there was something stranger waiting within those pages. British horror writer Dennis Wheatley was enjoying a renaissance around this time, his vintage tales of Satanism repackaged with lurid covers for the thrill-hungry '70s paperback market. So the Bond novels shared the shelves with such black magic chillers as The Devil Rides Out and The Haunting of Toby Jugg and all their delicious iconography of flaming skulls and pentagrams and sacrificial daggers. There was a weird, unspoken kinship between these books. Those shelves, I'm sure, ultimately took me to The War in the Dark and The Spider Dance.

Fleming always danced with the macabre. Like his friend Roald Dahl he had the blackest of imaginations and there's a flavour in his work that I like to describe as a scorpion-on-a-tombstone shudder (maybe that was another cover I saw, long ago...). And that sense of gilt-edged darkness nudges 007 tantalisingly close to Wheatley's world. Fleming's lexicon frequently borrows from the uncanny: the criminal organisation that Bond fights is called SPECTRE, after all (noun: a ghost; a phantom; an apparition). It's a word he was particularly partial to. From Russia With Love concerns a Soviet decoding machine called the Spektor. Diamonds Are Forever takes us to a Western ghost town named Spectreville. Elsewhere the killer in The Spy Who Loved Me, whose steel-capped teeth inspired the vampiric Jaws in the movie version, is named, simply, Horror.

Bond's underwater exploration in Thunderball is one of Fleming's finest pieces of writing, and there's a wonderful touch of Lovecraft to it. We enter the fuselage of a sunken plane, buried beneath the waves of the Bahamas. It holds the decomposing corpse of a crewman and, as we discover alongside Bond, it's infested with octopuses – "dreadful, glinting, red-eyed comets that slapped themselves into dark corners and stealthily squeezed themselves into cracks and under seats." The creatures, we're told, with skin-crawling understatement, have "a soft movement". It's the kind of prose that makes you wish he'd tapped out a full-blown horror novel on that gold-plated typewriter of his.

Two of the Bond books come tantalisingly close. Live and Let Die is the obvious one. Fleming's second novel, it's considerably pulpier than its predecessor, Casino Royale. In its pages Bond encounters the priestess Solitaire, who was initiated into the ways of voodoo during her childhood in Haiti. Intriguingly, she's presented to us as legitimately psychic, her powers exploited by the novel's villain, Mr Big. Voodoo lore permeates this mission, making it one of the more evocative Bond adventures, heavy with drums and sweat and superstition. Solitaire identifies "an ouanga, a Voodoo fetish. It's the invocation to the Drum Witch. It's used by the Ashanti tribe in Africa when they want to kill someone." Elsewhere we hear of a cursed island that's now regarded as "ju-ju". Mr Big himself is believed to be a manifestation of Baron Samedi, the spirit of darkness and death, or at least one of his zombie servants. The movie version amps up the horror angle, making the Baron a separate character, a cackling trickster figure who's strongly suggested to be an authentic supernatural force...

Published in 1964, less than five months before its author died, You Only Live Twice may just be Fleming's strangest, most genuinely haunting tale. In places it reads less like an espionage story and more like a fever dream, filled with symbolism and allegory. Bond is on the trail of his nemesis, Blofeld, who has retreated to Japan to create a Garden of Death. Seeded with poisonous plants and stocked with flesh-eating fish and lethal reptiles, it's a literal death trap, a magnet for a suicide cult that's sweeping the country. The Garden is an extraordinary idea, one of Fleming's most resonant, and it feels torn from fairytale or folklore, somewhere deeper and weirder than 007's usual international playground.

It's here, in this strange "killing bottle" of a location, that Bond faces mortality, just ahead of his creator: You only live twice, claims the quote that opens the book, once when you are born, and once when you look death in the face. It's a liminal space between this world and the other, edging Fleming's hero closer to the unknown.

Welcome to the shadow realm, Mr Bond. We've been expecting you.